nanci griffith's

other voices

A PERSONAL HISTORY OF FOLK MUSIC

NANCI GRIFFITH +
JOE JACKSON

Three Rivers Press
NEW YORK

Published by Three Rivers Press, a division of Crown Publishers, Inc.,
201 East 50th Street, New York, New York 10022.
Member of the Crown Publishing Group.

Random House, Inc. New York, Toronto, London, Sydney, Auckland
www.randomhouse.com

Three Rivers Press and colophon are trademarks of Crown Publishers, Inc.

DESIGN BY LYNNE AMFT

Printed in the United States of America

Library of Congress Cataloging-in-Publication Data
Griffith, Nanci.
Nanci Griffith's other voices : a personal history of folk music /
by Nanci Griffith and Joe Jackson.
1. Griffith, Nanci. 2. Popular music—History and criticism.
3. Folk Music—History and criticism. 4. Folk singers—United
States—Biography. I. Jackson, Joe. II. Title.
ML420.G859A3 1998
782.42164'092
[B]—DC21   98-19589

ISBN 0-609-80307-7

10 9 8 7 6 5 4 3 2 1

First Edition

To the memory
of all the voices in the choir
no longer earthbound of
this airwave....
We will sing your remembrance
often...loudly.

♪

Franklin, TN 1998

contents

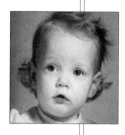

a c k n o w l e d g m e n t s

I would like to thank the following people for assistance with the management and production of this book: Ken Levitan, Kathi Whitley, Jim Rooney, Steve Ralbovsky, Nancy Covey, Nineyear Wooldridge, Alan Koenig, Burt Stein, Tammy Wise and everyone at Gold Mountain Entertainment, Richard Wootton, Claire Horton, Paul Charles and Asgard, Monterey Artists and Frank Riley, DNA and Rocky Schenck, Virginia Team, Alan Messer, and E. J. Camp.

And thanks to Chip Gibson, Steve Magnuson, Peter Guzzardi, Laurie Stark, Liana Faughnan, Lynne Amft, Mary Schuck, Jill Flaxman, Sibylle Kazeroid, Leta Evanthes, and everyone at the Crown Publishing Group.

Thank you to all of the record-label people everywhere: Dave Pennefeather, Marc Bell, MCA Records in the UK, East-West Records in the UK, Nancy Jeffreys, Sherry Ring Ginsberg, Dane Venable, Lisa Michaelson and everyone at Elektra Records, everyone at WEA Worldwide, Almo-Irving Music, David Conrad, Lance Freed, and Rondor Music International.

For assistance with research, we're grateful to Bill Ivy and Kyle Young of the (Nashville) Country Music Foundation, the Stephen Foster Story and Barbie Bryant in Bardstown, Kentucky, the Stephen Foster Memorial, University of Pittsburgh, Dr. Deane Root, David Gahr, the Guthrie Foundation, Marlin Griffith, Brian Wood and Mickie Merkins, Carolyn Hester, Pete Seeger, Odetta, Rod Kennedy and the Kerrville Music Foundation, and Jeanene Van Zandt

All of the people who helped in the recording and technical aspects of making *Other Voices . . .* have earned our gratitude: Jack's Tracks, Nashville—Mark Miller; Scream Studio, L.A.—Don Gehman and Doug Trantow; Woodland Studio, Nashville—Chris Stone; Windmill Land Studio, Dublin—Brian Masterson and Ciaran Cahill; Georgetown Mastering, Nashville—Denny Purcell; Back Pocket Studio, New York—Joe Arlotta and Gerry Volkersz.

And thanks to everyone who provided me with friendship and support over the years: Susanna Clark, Tish Hinojosa, Gloria Steinem, Ray Kennedy and Steve Earle, Lucinda Williams, Julie Gold, Eric and Martha Taylor, Tom Russell, Stuart Duncan, Nina Gerber, Odetta, Tom and Jackie Littlefield, Elaine Peterson, Chris Noth, Sonny and Louise Curtis, J. I. and Joanie Allison, Joe B. and Jane Mauldin, Frank Christian, Al Bunetta and John Prine, Oh Boy Records, Paul Kennerly, Susan Cowsill, Peter Holsapple, Darius Rucker and Fishco, the Van Zandt family, those Harris Women, Joy Lewallen, the Blue Moon Orchestra, Jim Rooney, and Jessica Schulte.

—*Nanci Griffith*

nanci griffith's
other
voices

foreword

There's a moment in *The Fountainhead,* Ayn Rand's master-work, where the hero, the architect Roark, stands high above the city, atop a building he designed. Roark high in his aerie symbolizes one central thesis of Rand's work: the power of one determined individual to change events, to be a force for good, can be greater than the collective power of thousands. To me there's a lot of Roark in Nanci Griffith, a delightful mixture of elfin grace, Texas charm, a ready smile, and a steel will.

I've been following her career since at least the mid-1970s, and I've watched her very closely since I heard her gloriously wonderful *Once in a Very Blue Moon* album, released originally on Philo/Rounder in 1984. Griffith has now created *Other Voices, Too,* her fifteenth album, this one accompanied by this collaborative book, written with Joe Jackson, which eloquently describes the participating songs, singers, and musicians.

Nanci's a small-boned woman with a fully developed motel tan, a slender brunette almost waiflike in appearance,

15

someone who probably wouldn't win many arm-wrestling contests but who's hard to beat in a battle of will or wits. Love and happiness, warmth and compassion, always ride shotgun with Nanci, who has companions down every road, sidekicks for all seasons.

She started her (still ongoing) growing-up process when she was born in Seguin, Texas (pop. 16,418), the Guadalupe County seat. Before long the family moved to Austin, the state capital and home to the huge University of Texas, a vortex of intellectual activity and turmoil. During summers Nanci visited her grandparents in Lockney (pop. 2,232), halfway between two county seats, one in Plainview, the other in Floydada. That's way out in west Texas, tumbleweed territory, and like the spinning, whirling plant, Nanci has been freewheeling through life on a trip between hither and yon, lighting for brief periods during her years in Austin and in her residencies in Nashville and Dublin, before heading out once again. As a result of her journeying she has developed a substantial following—beyond a cult, a few arenas shy of superstardom—in the United States, Canada, and Europe. During a recording career that began in 1976 on B. F. Deal Records, Nanci has tried various musical styles, from traditional folk right on into country, pop, and rock. *Other Voices, Too* returns her to her original, and many feel her most convincing, role—that of the wandering troubadour. Come to think of it, that's the role chosen by most of the songwriters represented in this album as well as those who contributed tunes to this set's Grammy-winning predecessor, *Other Voices, Other Rooms*.

Like the ad for the brokerage firm, Nanci Griffith achieved prominence, secured major label recording deals, and received five Grammy nominations the old-fashioned way: she earned them. She paid her dues and, I suspect, probably paid dues for a few others, too. Along about 1976 she strung up her guitar, topped off her Toyota, and embarked on a solo road trip that lasted ten years. That's ten years of living alone in tawdry rooms in cheap hotels, more than 3,650 days of ingesting road food, about 100,000 hours spent nearly always in motion, mostly with only the muse for company, going to one show, setting up the next and the next and the next until one day in 1986 Nanci realized that ten years and about a million miles had passed.

So she made the only logical move she could: she hired a band. Since that day of decision the Blue Moon Orchestra has joined her on her journeys and if you want to know why they are around, just listen to how beautifully they build a musical foundation for Nanci and other celebrated folksingers to embellish with their voices. Take a bow James Hooker (keyboards, vocals), Ron de la Vega (bass, cello, vocals), Doug Lancio (electric guitar), Lee Satterfield (guitar, mandolin, vocals), and Pat McInerney (drums and percussion).

I always associate the word "character" with Nanci, not in the sense of "she's really a character" but as in "she's really got character." In Texas, where I also grew up, "character" means grit, individuality, integrity, and heart. It also strikes me that Nanci is remarkably other-directed, more so than almost any performer I've ever met. When she asks, "How're you doing?" she really wants to know; she sincerely does care about life beyond ego.

In that regard, one of my favorite Nanci stories concerns what she said when she announced she would record and tour with the Crickets, the backup trio for Buddy Holly but—by the mid-1990s, let's face it—a group far beneath her standing as a contemporary star. Now, she could have made a long-winded speech, or she could have, like many of today's artists, said something incomprehensible. Instead she simply said, "Ever since I was a little girl I've wanted to be a Cricket." Then, on record and on tour, she walked it like she talked it, inviting the Crickets into her set and onto her record and joining their live performance so that the Crickets got equal billing as part of a celebratory show; they were not simply a supporting act. That's called giving back, and there are tears welling up in my eyes now as I recall Nanci's actions and consider how few artists take the trouble to acknowledge and salute their influences so openly and with such feeling.

Another mark of Nanci's character is that instead of releasing an album consisting predominantly of her own material, as she did on twelve of her last thirteen CDs, she has again chosen, as in 1993's *Other Voices, Other Rooms,* to present some of her favorite songs, songs that she grew up hearing, songs that pierced her heart, songs that lent her strength to continue along the trail. Thus Nanci Griffith is not only dressing these nineteen songs in a new suit of 1998 clothes; she's also paying heartfelt tribute and sincere homage to the men and women who wrote them, a cast ranging from one of America's greatest songwriters, Stephen Foster, who died penniless in 1864, to heroes of previous "folk booms": Woody Guthrie; Pete Seeger; Tom Rush; Eric Von Schmidt; Peter, Paul and Mary; right up to contemporary writer-performers such as Richard Thompson, Tom Russell, Guy Clark, and Pat McLaughlin.

The overall brilliance of the *Other Voices* projects made me curious. How come folk music has gotten the shaft all these years, except during the late 1950s folk boom? I suspect there are some purists who believe that folk music, true folk music, started to die in 1920, when radio made it possible for thousands of people in disparate locations to hear a song, a speech, or a commercial simultaneously. Suddenly the old method of face-to-face dissemination of songs changed to an impersonal one, with radio replacing direct personal contact.

And over the years, as new musical forms were created and marketed, and as new radio formats were launched, each pushed the lonesome folksinger farther into the background, a dispiriting process for the troubadours, particularly in view of the fact that they, not their trendy, more visible colleagues in rock, pop, and rap, were keeping the music alive, passing the torch burning with yesterday's songs to the singers of tomorrow.

Somewhere along the line the dictators of cool, the arbiters of trend, decided folk music was too boring or maybe too hard to market, or perhaps they were secretly envious. At any rate, they recast a few selected folksingers as singer-songwriters, anointed them as saints of pain and angst, and heaped praise on their every utterance. Meanwhile the remaining folksingers were deemed anachronistic voices from the past, lonesome figures wailing away to small audiences, treated like lovable but slightly loopy cousins at a family reunion.

Maybe folksingers got left behind because as a rule they are more selfless than most performers, more interested in drawing people's attention and passion to injustices and to issues than to their own circumstances. They aren't usually very good at marketing and self-promotion.

What's the difference between a folksinger and a commercially successful singer-songwriter like Paul Simon, Tracy Chapman, Michael Stipe, Jewel, or Ani DiFranco? All write and sing music that they feel passionate enough about to record and present: slices from their own lonely introspection served up for public inspection.

What, when you get right down to it, separates Kurt Cobain from a folksinger? Granted he chose to present his songs in the context of a small band setting, but aren't Cobain's songs, stripped of their electricity, the folk songs of his life and his generation?

In its simplest form, folk music is a passionate, living, breathing view of today's world through the eyes and ears of the folksinger. There's nothing musty, dusty, old, or anachronistic about the art; it's as current as cyberspace, as basic as black. The spirit, the soul, that is the heart of folk music lives on in Nanci and in the contributors here. They still go out of town far too often to suit those who love them. And they still play music they have created and learned for roomfuls of strangers, hoping, like troubadours always, to spread a little joy, to make people think, to entertain, and to suspend for their audience, if only for a brief time, the woes that are so much with them.

When I listen to Nanci Griffith, I hear a national treasure, a walking, talking embodiment of all that is good about folk music. For over twenty years she has been a carrier of the torch passed from such luminaries as Joan Baez, Judy Collins, and Carolyn Hester. Nanci has kept the torch lit and has passed it triumphantly along to others. Ten, fifteen, twenty years from now we will read of some sensational new singing star who will tell us how they, like Darius Rucker of Hootie and the Blowfish, were inspired by seeing and hearing Nanci Griffith perform and thinking to themselves, Someday I'm going to do that, by golly! (Rucker recently had his dream come true when he recorded a duet with Nanci on her own song, "Gulf Coast Highway," on her last album, *Blue Roses from the Moons*.)

I think that to me Nanci stands for what America originally meant, a country built around free thought, a nation founded by mavericks so averse to ignorant or arbitrary authority that they sailed across a perilous ocean to an unsettled, dangerous land so they could be free to live without interference. Ironically, when I think of the elfin Nanci, who somehow also reminds me of Tinker Bell, forever scattering magical musical pixie dust in her wake, I think first of two words: "rugged" and "individualist."

The world needs a lot more people like Nanci Griffith: long may she live, sing, and share her life with us!

—John Lomax III, 1998

preface by
nanci griffith

They were a couple of beat punk kids from West Texas: my mother of platinumed hair always pulled back to a high French twist, dressed in black turtleneck sweaters with straight gray wool skirts; my father, tall and thin, with pomped jet-black hair, sharp of long sideburns, dressed in pegged trousers and crisp white shirts. They were totally beautiful, both of them.

They were an uncommon pair for their time and place, and yet they were the definition of an American art form and the American dream. Born of ancestors from Scotland and Wales, so dark and familial in tradition, transported to the flatland dust bowl of the panhandle of West Texas, which had been ravaged and swept clean by the dust storms of the Great Depression. They found each other in the midst of this devastation, fresh in their love, within the 1940s Austin, Texas, intellectual beat generation.

No one has ever been truly able to fully explain the exact origins of the post–World War II beat generation. They came

Nanci Griffith
KERRVILLE
FOLK
FESTIVAL,
1981

*photo by
Brian
Kanof*

21

into their individualism as adolescents during those war years. Too young to fight in the war and too old to enjoy a carefree childhood, they were the original Generation X, Rebels Without a Cause for the late twentieth century. They were somewhat of a lost generation searching for their own identities in a land of revived national confidence, "I Like Ike," and the unresolved Korean Conflict.

Their generation gave birth to the majority of today's American population, the baby boomers, the largest population explosion in American history. They gave us their own voice of dissent within the existentialism of the Beat movement. The Beat voices expressed concern for civilization, harmony, and reform in the racial melting pot of America with the beginnings of the civil rights movement. They were the first American generation to look outward from America with a global sense of responsibility for the future.

My father was a printer and graphic artist by trade whose true love was traditional music and singing harmony in the pure Welsh tenor voice passed on to him by his father and his grandfather before him in the form of woodshedding, which is now referred to as barbershop quartet singing. He can actually read antiquated songbooks, hymnals, and choral arrangements written in shape notes, which provide a code of sorts to let a musician understand the relationship between notes in a song, thereby allowing for easy transposition into different keys.

He has always challenged me to believe there is nothing musical on this earth that I cannot understand if I just take the time to listen. He will always remain one of my true inspirations, not only for his passion for preserving what has been written in music history but also for encouraging me as a young songwriter and teaching me the importance of listening to the songs written by my peers. I have always admired his respect for new voices. Without his love for contemporary songwriters, I would probably never have heard the music of writers such as Townes Van Zandt and Guy Clark. Listening and learning from such incredibly gifted writers was as instrumental in helping me hone my own songwriting skills as was finding my own voice and inspiration.

My father passed his love and respect for music and literature on to all three of his children. His hi-fi was his joy, from traditional music to Appalachian Mountain music to Woody Guthrie, Odetta, Dave Van Ronk, and Carolyn Hester, back to Leadbelly and off to Pete Seeger and the

Weavers for a time to the musical interpretations of songs from the 1800s recorded by the Carter Family. His greatest love, along with the songbooks he collected, has always been the songs of Stephen Collins Foster. Many of the songs I've included in the two volumes of *Other Voices* I learned from my father, including Foster's "Hard Times Come Again No More," and from *Other Voices, Other Rooms,* G. P. Cook and Ralph Roland's "Are You Tired of Me, My Darling," which captured so simply and beautifully a woman's fears and dreams in a woman's voice in 1877.

I'm sure that in reality, my father never thought any of his children were listening. We *were* listening, though, and from him we learned Stephen Foster's "Hard Times," inspired by Charles Dickens's novel of the same title. Foster's song colorfully illustrated and gave heart with a melody to the depression in Europe and the potato famine in Ireland of the 1850s.

Through the traditional song "Wasn't That a Mighty Storm," adapted by Tom Rush and Eric Von Schmidt, we learned through a musical oral history about the great hurricane of Galveston Island, Texas, on a Saturday afternoon, September 8, 1900, which took thousands of lives in its fury and totally destroyed the port of entry that my ancestors had come through to America in the mid-1800s. Through these songs I hear the voice of my father, his father, my grandmothers. These songs are a sound track for social history, thankfully available to us all for the spending and collecting throughout our lives complete with the tradition and joy of passing them on to the next generation.

The most treasured gift my father ever gave me is a book by Alan Lomax, *Folk Songs of North America.* It is an incredible collection of musical history that I have referred to like a bible throughout my life. My two recorded volumes of *Other Voices* are a mere tip of the iceberg compared to Lomax's lifework of collecting and preserving folk music.

My mother, in all her rebellion, loved jazz and big band music. She gave us Dave Brubeck, Count Basie, and Woody Herman. Frank Sinatra rang with bells in our house. That was her time on the hi-fi, and you didn't impose on that dream time of my mother's. It was her space, and we were children and as far as she was concerned, we could never understand where she was within that music. She thought it was an adult thing.

More than my father, she embraced the Beat philosophy and lifestyle. She taught her children to respect people's differences and to place no limits upon ourselves in our life goals. As my parents matured, my mother traveled

The Griffith Family Back Porch Jamboree
1954

Nanci is the infant in her aunt Nell's lap, far right; Nanci's sister, Mikki, is seated next to Aunt Nell. Marlin "Grif" Griffith, Nanci's dad, is seated front center; Nanci's mom, Rue, is next to him. Percy Griffith (Nanci's grandfather) is wearing a hat and seated front right. Her grandmother, Sue, is front left with Nanci's brother, Robert, in her lap.

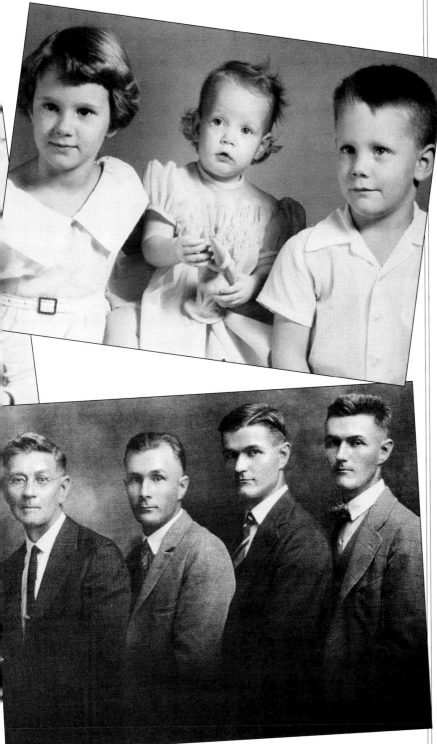

Those Griffith Kids
1 9 5 6

left to right:
Marlene (Mikki), 9;
Nanci, 20 months;
Robert, 8

The Griffith Quartet
1 9 2 8

left to right:
Rev. W. G. Griffith
(Nanci's great-grandfather),
Percy Griffith (Nanci's
grandfather), Elmer Griffith,
Steven Griffith (the twins—
Nanci's great-uncles). The
quartet was well known in the
central Texas area and west of
Austin in the '20s and '30s.
Rev. Griffith would preach
and the quartet would sing
to the congregation.

photos from
Nanci Griffith's
personal collection

far to the left and my father moved to the right of that mythical American center, resulting in their separation and divorce in 1960. After their divorce, my mother became more involved with her artistic passions, dabbling in acting at the Austin Civic Theatre, attending poetry readings, literary clubs, and music jamborees at Austin's first Beat coffeehouse on Sixth Street, the Red Lion, which was owned by a dear friend of our family, John Meadows.

I played my first professional engagement at the Red Lion at age twelve on a Thanksgiving night when the act originally booked canceled. I made eleven dollars and cleared the already small house with my poor performance, but it was a start, which my mother remains very proud to have provided. She remarried during that same year to jazz pianist Eddie George, whose real name is George Strawser. George had played with Woody Herman's big band in 1953 and 1954—before Woody cut his big band down to a combo. Some of my fondest memories are of hanging over the piano bars my stepfather played and requesting song after song, trying to stump him—which I could never do. All those hi-fi days of my mother's came back to mind as I hovered over his piano, and those songs she assumed we weren't interested in came to my voice.

Though I often wished my parents were more "normal," in a conventional sense, I am also grateful that they maintained their passion for the arts and did not abandon that love by conforming to the average endeavors enjoyed by the typical American family in the 1950s and through my childhood in the 1960s. While most of my friends' parents centered their lives on the hobbies and passions of their children, my parents and their peers expected their children to center their lives on the activities of the parents. Who's to say which approach gives the most to children? But I am forever grateful for the enlightenment of my parents' love of literature, theatre, music, and art, and for the company of their diverse and intriguing friends.

I would not trade my teenage memory of my father taking me to hear Townes Van Zandt for the first time in a small club in Austin for anything "normal." It was on that night that I first heard Townes's "Tecumseh Valley." That song forever changed my life and lent me character and strength. The song was about a young woman named Caroline whose sadness and departure from life rested in the absence of choice for her own future. My middle name is Caroline, so as an impressionable young woman I took Caroline's story to heart. Thinking about her downfall and sorrow often saved me from making wrong turns when I felt I had no choice but to do so. When on my

Marlin Griffith

1 9 9 2

Taken during the
"Wimoweh" recording for
Other Voices, Other Rooms

Ruelene, Nanci's mom

1 9 9 3

The Other Voices, Other
Rooms *Tour, Austin, Texas*

photos from
Nanci Griffith's
personal collection

own I did choose to turn the wrong way, her story gave me strength to get up and move on, knowing I had the ability to create my own choices and exercise my own free will.

We are all but the reflection of our individual choices. Music has always been the one common grace of our own personal lives. It is a point to which we discipline ourselves and where we diverge and totally reserve unto individuals. It's a total and secret identity we can all hold as our own.

I borrowed the title *Other Voices, Other Rooms* from Truman Capote's first novel, published in 1948. That book heralded a host of new voices in literature and coincided with a rebirth of interest in folk music, with the added twist of focus on the singer-songwriter. Woody Guthrie, Pete Seeger, the Almanac Singers, Alan Lomax, the Weavers, the Carter Family, and Odetta, among others, were true pioneers in passing on the passion of the singer-songwriter to the next generation. Folk music has had a couple of revivals since that first wave. The spotlight has remained on the brilliance of the voice of the songwriter, who captures lyrically and musically a panoramic view of the social climate and the writer's sense of place for the next of us to hear and sing in the voice of our own time.

As a young child in Austin, Texas, in the early 1960s, I became physically attached and addicted to my transistor radio. It set me free to consume batteries and make my own choices about the music I wanted to hear. Folk and dust bowl rock and roll became my first love. Carolyn Hester's voice through my transistor radio gave me wings to fly and a place to be. Buddy Holly and the Crickets wrote their own songs and were the first group of rockers with roots in bluegrass and hillbilly folk music to be so self-reliant and complete.

My first recollection of television is of my family gathering around my grandparents' TV in 1958 to watch the Crickets on *The Ed Sullivan Show.* Though Buddy Holly died in a plane crash in 1959, his influence with the Crickets set a precedent for the future of popular music. The Crickets continued to write their own songs, cut their own records, play their own instruments, and write brilliant songs for others. Sonny Curtis, Jerry "J.I." Allison, and Joe B. Mauldin of the Crickets remain well-sung heroes whose writing continues to influence and find new voices. Paul McCartney has said they were the main inspiration for the Beatles and for the name of the group. Sonny Curtis's song "Walk Right Back," which was a hit for the Everly Brothers in 1961, was the easiest song to record for *Other Voices, Too,* perhaps because the Crickets were there to play with me and Sonny was there to sing harmony, but also because I'd been singing that song in my young dreams for all those years of having the transistor radio glued to my ear.

Radio still had an innocence then, which allowed a child in Austin, Texas, to hear Carolyn Hester back-to-back with the Everly Brothers and Nat "King" Cole, followed by a Weavers song. Music didn't need to fit into a neat category in order to be heard. Without that open ear of radio, I would never have found my own muses or my own voice, nor would I have dreamed of becoming a songwriter writing songs for other voices to sing. That open format of radio gave us the diversity and integrity of Bob Dylan, whose voice I first heard coming full blast from my sister's stereo through the wall adjoining our bedrooms. Hence my recording of his song "Boots of Spanish Leather" for *Other Voices, Other Rooms*.

Unfortunately we have now lost that open ear of radio format and the clarity of diverse programming. Where once we had radio disc jockeys who brought their own taste and wacky personalities into the station along with the best of what could be heard, we now have dictated formats with narrow myopic song playlists that must fit tightly into some corporate category for each station. DJs no longer have control of their personalities or their own soundboards. Radio has become so homogenized that it has no vitamins, no minerals, no nourishment, and no sharp edges. In the nineties we've an entire generation of children who have never heard any type of music but what they hear on their particular rock or country station, and never do any two paths cross. It's as boring and mundane as being forced to watch a whole summer of television sitcom reruns.

We've also entered a frightful time in education where funds for music and the arts in our schools are being drastically reduced, as well as funding to Public Broadcasting, which has so often been the great champion of alternative genres of music not often heard on commercial formats.

It's been my intention in this project to pass on these songs and voices to the next of us in search of their first musical love, and to preserve, as best I could, the phrasing and individuality of all the songwriters in the two volumes of *Other Voices*. I harbor great hopes that those who hear these songs for the first time, and discover a genre of music they'd like to hear more of, will go out to the record store and search through the bins to find the original works of these writers and artists.

There are so many writers whose songs I wanted to record for these albums that I am at a loss as to how I can express my true affection and admiration for their work. My co-producer, Jim Rooney, was most patient with me and instrumental in helping me choose the songs I could interpret best from my incredibly long song list. Missing are songs by John Stewart, Loretta Lynn, Don Everly, Phil Everly, Paul Siebel, Mary McCaslin, Joni Mitchell, Phil Ochs, Rosalie Sorrels, Michael Martin Murphy, Bill Stains, Paul Kennerly, Leonard Cohen, Judy Collins, Richard Leigh, Butch Hancock, Robert Earl Keen Jr., Jimmie Dale Gilmore, Paul Simon, Jackson Browne, Susanna Clark, Bob McDill, Richard Dobson, Richard Fariña (Carolyn Hester's first husband and writer of the cult classic novel *Been Down So Long, It Looks Like Up to Me*), Joe Ely, Emmylou Harris, John Gorka, Greg Brown, Shawn Colvin, Jimmy Webb, Lucinda Williams, Cindy Walker, James Taylor, Carole King, and so many more. Perhaps someday . . .

Kind thanks to all these generations of singers, players, and songwriters who made space in their busy schedules to gather together for this project and lend their voices to these songs. Carolyn Hester said it best in that she'd arrived with Arlo Guthrie into a very special folk festival. It was such an incredible honor to be in the company of my heroes of such enormous talent whose mutual love of this music gave this project heart and wings to fly. And to all the artists Jim Rooney and I felt belonged on this project and who tried their best to get here but whose schedules simply would not permit—Billy Bragg, Norman and Nancy Blake, Patty Larkin, and Christine Lavin, to name a few—thanks for trying. We missed you and thought of your voices, and perhaps someday . . . Last but not least, thanks to Iris DeMent, Lee Satterfield, and Gillian Welch, who so remind me of my own self as a young woman songwriter out driving myself around America to play music.

Throughout our recording sessions in Nashville, New York, Los Angeles, and Dublin, Ireland, I've had the incredible opportunity of seeing a lifelong dream come true for me as both an artist and a songwriter. With the first volume of *Other Voices, Other Rooms,* we had the chance to celebrate more traditional folk music, along with a few contemporary songwriters. With *Other Voices, Too: A Trip Back to Bountiful,* we had an opportunity to explore a time in music when folk and rock merged without effort or fear of being labeled. At the end of the day these two volumes, recorded from 1993 to 1998, have been a gathering of artists, voices, musicians, and songwriters of all generations and musical categories to celebrate this common heritage of music, and it truly has been a trip back to bountiful and a brilliant gift to pass on to the next generation.

I am grateful for the collaboration on the text for this book with my friend, journalist Joe Jackson. Joe writes regularly for the *Irish Times* and *Hot Press* out of Dublin, Ireland, and for many music publications worldwide. He is the rare music journalist who actually listens to music. His knowledge as a musicologist has been treasured and invaluable to this project. His contribution to this text is deeply appreciated as well as the time he took out from working on his own book to come to America to work with me and to interview all the artists quoted here.

Like DJs of a generation ago, music journalists who are also great writers are few and far between these days. I hope that contemporary music will always maintain writers like Joe Jackson in Ireland and the UK and America's own Steve Morse who writes full time for the *Boston Globe* and freelance for many national publications. Without these writers and their rare peers we might never see another book like *Folks Songs of North America* from an archivist the likes of its writer, Alan Lomax. I also appreciate John Lomax, in keeping with the tradition of his family's history as writers and archivists, taking the time, talent, and knowledge to write the foreword for this book. His words are sacred to me as an artist.

ABOUT THE PHOTOGRAPHS

When I first began work on these recording projects, the thought crossed my mind that it would be wonderful to present these songs of these most treasured songwriters not only by the preservation of the integrity of their work but also by seeking a visual image that captures the writer at the approximate time when the song was written. To that purpose I referred back to a lovely book, *The Face of Folk Music,* with photographs by David Gahr and text by Robert Shelton, published in 1968 by Citadel Press in New York. I also revisited my co-producer, Jim Rooney's book, *Baby, Let Me Follow You Down,* a history of the New England and New York folk scene revival of the 1960s and early 1970s, which he co-wrote with Eric Von Schmidt, as well as Rooney's *Bossmen: Bill Monroe and Muddy Waters.*

David Gahr has been the man with the eye and the camera in his hand for the past half century in roots music. He has been the main contributor of archival photographs for the album sleeves and booklets. His photos are works of art. We all see and wonder of how he actually captured the voices in the writers' faces. David also has a photographic memory, and he tells

Nanci and the Crickets
left to right:
Joe B. Mauldin, Nanci
Griffith, J. I. Allison, Sonny
Curtis
1997

photo by
Raeanne Rubenstein

Nanci Griffith and
J. I. Allison
1996

photo by Alan Messer

Bill and Bonnie Hearne
1997

photo by Alan Messer

left to right:
Odetta, James Hooker,
John Gorka
1993

photo by Beth Gwinn

Nanci Griffith and Harlan
Howard
NASHVILLE, 1997

photo by Alan Messer

wonderful stories while he shoots his work. I never tire of his humor, his wit, and his energy. You generally know you've arrived on the folk scene when David takes your picture, and that's a true honor.

Photographer Jim "Señor" McGuire has made incredible contributions as well. Though he hasn't been shooting as long as David, he has been one of the most sought-after visual artists in the Nashville folk, country, and bluegrass music scene for the last twenty years. He has shot album covers for me, John Prine, Guy Clark, Townes Van Zandt, Jamie Hartford, John Hartford, Rodney Crowell, Emmylou Harris, Bill Monroe, Harlan Howard, and a list of others too long to attempt to mention. He shares that same artistic eye behind the camera as David and is able to magically capture our melodies in our faces. McGuire is currently at work on his own book of photographs.

For the live recording sessions on the first volume I came loaded with my own camera to each session as well as bringing in a Nashville photographer, Beth Gwinn, whose work regularly appears in *People Magazine* and many other national publications. Beth has an extraordinary sense of humor and has the delightful and unique gift of bringing out the bright side of even the darkest and most intense of us. She has an uncanny ability to catch us on film doing things that totally contradict our perceived nature. For example, her photograph of Odetta, John Gorka, and the bandleader of my Blue Moon Orchestra, James Hooker, huddled together reading a national tabloid magazine is priceless, spontaneous, and an activity you would never catch any one of them doing individually. Her photos make me laugh out loud. Her greatest contribution to all of this work is showing you and reminding me, in her visual art, how much fun we all had during these recording sessions. The love that was gathered there was a genuine smile for us all.

When we started recording the second volume of *Other Voices* in the winter of 1996, we traveled to several locations other than just Nashville. I had been working with British photographer Alan Messer, whose work I have admired for many years. Alan's own history in music is awe inspiring, including working with the Beatles. Alan was a blessing for the recordings in Nashville, New York, Austin, and Los Angeles. While we were recording, he had a most selfless way of moving through the actual recording studio and capturing our performance without any of us being particularly aware of his presence or his camera. He put up with very long sessions, hard travelin', and natural candlelight in the studio, and through it all he remained in great spirits and, when not invisible, gave us much cheer.

Nollaig Casey
DUBLIN, 1997

photo by
Gerry O'Leary

Dolores Keane
DUBLIN, 1997

photo by
Gerry O'Leary

Mickie Merkins
and Brian Wood
1982

photo by
Tad Hershorn

Alan took a gorgeous portrait of the folk duo Bill and Bonnie Hearne, who were a great inspiration for me in my early years and who also play the best darn folk music I've ever heard. Bill's eyesight is severely impaired, and Bonnie is blind. On a lovely day out at my farm during the sessions when several folks came to visit, including Bill and Bonnie, Alan shot a photo of the two of them walking hand in hand along my clothesline, with bed linens billowing in the wind around them and musicians following behind them. It is one of my most treasured possessions and is a beautiful visual expression of this project. The majority of the session photos here in the book are Alan's. He also shot the cover for my last album, *Blue Roses from the Moons*. We all feel very proud to have worked with Alan for over a year on all these sessions and travels. I thank him for his patience and apologize for the occasional outburst of "Get outta my face with that camera!"

Alan could not be with us in Dublin, but he recommended a photographer there by the name of Gerry O'Leary. The Dublin sessions were incredibly eerie and surreal. Working with my band, as in all the sessions, but also having the magic of guest musicians Nollaig Casey and Mary Custy on violins, Sharon Shannon on accordion, and the legendary Delores Keane on harmony vocals. All of these women are the best of Irish musicians whom we have respected and anticipated recording with for years. We overwhelmed ourselves by also bringing in from London Iain Matthews, formerly of Richard Thompson's Fairport Convention, on guitar and harmony; Clive Gregson, also on guitar and harmony; Brian Willoughby, of the Strawbs, on acoustic guitar extraordinaire; and the spine-rumbling bass vocals of Tom Russell, who came in from New York. Brian Masterson engineered these sessions as well as sessions we had recorded for the first volume there in Dublin. Perhaps it is a spell he casts on us with the sounds he gave our voices, or maybe it was the atmosphere of his studio there or the nature of the material we were recording with such uniquely talented musicians that created a glow of light around everyone.

"Who Knows Where the Time Goes" is a particular favorite of mine, written by another of my early heroes, the late Sandy Denny, who was also a member of Richard Thompson's Fairport Convention. That song brought us all to tears, fluttered the flames in the candles, and sent chills through all of us with Delores Keane's voice coming up through the Irish earth through the soles (soul) of her feet and out through the microphone. It left us all speechless, knowing that something beyond all our talent and comprehension had just been recorded and had consumed us all.

If I believed in ghosts or spirits I would have sworn that the spirit of Sandy Denny and that of Stephen Foster, whose song "Hard Times Come Again No More" we recorded later that evening to the same fascination, had joined us in the form of that flutter in the candle's flame and the odd glow of light around us. Gerry O'Leary caught the whole session on film, so we know we did not imagine it. In his quiet, unassuming manner Gerry worked around the cables and the clutter of so many musicians playing in a small studio space. His photographs are stunning. The most delicate and surreal photo is the one we chose for the inside back cover of this book and the inside dedication sleeve of the CD booklet of *Other Voices, Too: A Trip Back to Bountiful.* Gerry shot this photo of Jim Rooney and me listening to the playback of these two songs through the glass between the engineering console and the studio, and the glow of light surrounding us is clearly visible. That was one of the two most haunting moments in my recording experience.

The other haunting recording session for me happened in Nashville during the sessions for the first volume. We were recording "Across the Great Divide," written by the late Kate Wolf who had been a dear friend as well as a songwriter whose work I deeply admired. Kate and I have very different voices: she had a soft angelic voice that always seemed almost a whisper while my voice is all highs and edges. When we recorded "Across the Great Divide," I could hear Kate's voice as I sang instead of my own, as though she took over for a while. Five years later I still hear Kate's voice when I listen to that recording.

Most of the photos of me and guitarist Brian Wood, from early in my career and during my first national tour in 1982 with Carolyn Hester, were taken by my friend Wayne Miller, who often traveled with us. Brian's wife, Mickie Merkins, wrote "Yarrington Town," about a young girl's coming-of-age, which we recorded on *Other Voices, Too.* The experience of recording this song as a trio with Emmylou Harris and Carolyn Hester—along with Emmy's daughter, Meghan, and Carolyn's daughters, Amy and Carla, singing harmony—was both an enlightening and endearing moment for me as an artist. That song truly belongs to these two mothers in their message, through Mickie's lyrics, to their daughters. If every mother went into parenthood of daughters equipped with Mickie's song "Yarrington Town" and Malvina Reynolds and Harry Belafonte's classic song "Turn Around," which we recorded on the first volume of *Other Voices,* I think they'd do a fine job of passing on a voice of wisdom.

In fact, James Hooker, who has three daughters of his own, says these two songs make him wish he had more daughters just so he could sing 'em to them.

ABOUT THE BLUE MOON ORCHESTRA

When I think of musicologists and archivists I usually imagine someone like myself. Someone thick of eyeglass wandering somewhat aimlessly among the stacks of their particular fascination. My band, the Blue Moon Orchestra, doesn't exactly fit into that image. The Blue Moon Orchestra was formed during the Christmas holidays of 1986 as a band of musicians who could work the road tours as well as pass effortlessly through the minefields of incredibly diverse recording sessions. Each one of the musicians brought to our band an expertise that has resulted in a distinctive sound. They chose their name from my 1984 album, *Once in a Very Blue Moon.* They are each uniquely gifted in their particular instruments, as well as being the most wonderful wall of sound as a group. The alumni list of my band always amazes me, and I feel most fortunate to have shared my music and the road with all of them throughout these years. We are individuals of different musical genres, ages, and interests, yet somehow we are cast of the same mold, and that in itself has created a consistent magic for these sessions.

Philip Donnelly, who is originally from Dublin, Ireland, started playing with me in 1984. Philip has the most unusual style of any guitarist I've heard. He has lent that "special and winged" guitar style, which we've dubbed "seagull guitar," to many artists, including Donovan, John Prine, the Everly Brothers, and Maura O'Connell. I learned Ralph McTell's song "From Clare to Here" from Philip.

South Carolinian James Hooker has been our original fearless leader since 1986. As with Philip, he brings his unique style of musical technique with him whether he is on piano, synthesizer, B-3 organ, celeste, or harmonium. No matter what he plays, it is always distinctly recognizable as James Hooker. He has been the sound for some of music's most memorable recordings, playing B-3 organ for Al Green, as a founding member of country-rock pioneers the Amazing Rhythm Aces, and a co-writer touring with Steve Winwood. In addition to his keyboard work in the band, he has

Nanci Griffith and Brian Wood

KERRVILLE FOLK
FESTIVAL, 1982

photo by Wayne Miller

Three Young Women
l e f t   t o   r i g h t :
Carla Blum (Carolyn Hester's daughter), Meghan Ahern (Emmylou Harris's daughter), Amy Blum (Carolyn's daughter)
1 9 9 7

"Yarrington Town"
photo by Alan Messer

The Blue Moon Orchestra
l e f t   t o   r i g h t :
Nanci Griffith, Lee Satterfield, Pat McInerney, Ron de la Vega, Doug Lancio, James Hooker
1 9 9 7

photo by
Alan Messer

also been my only co-writer in the Blue Moon Orchestra, and he is a most formidable duet singer. He is the heart and soul of this band.

Pat McInerney, originally from Hemel Hempstead, England, came to America from the British folk-rock scene playing drums and percussion with Don Williams. He can turn almost anything into a rhythm instrument to play with a finesse and flair rare to the breed of musicians who are responsible for hitting on things. He has become the definitive percussionist/drummer of Nashville alternative session players. He is as much at home playing with me for a symphony concert as he is in a dingy punk club, and he's one of the few drummers you'd ever find who will ask for a lyric sheet to a song. Pat and I share a deep affection for the early music of Fairport Convention with Richard Thompson, Iain Matthews, and Sandy Denny and for groups like the Crickets, the Seldom Scene, Chesapeake, and the Strawbs. His musical influence on our band is obvious and indispensable.

I met our second drummer, Fran Breen, through Philip Donnelly in Dublin in 1987. I had recorded Julie Gold's extraordinary world anthem, "From a Distance," in 1986 for my *Lone Star State of Mind* album. It became an immediate number one hit in Ireland, which initiated many tours for me and the band in Ireland, the United Kingdom, and throughout Europe.

On a visit to Ireland to record for the television program *Sessions,* Philip introduced me to Fran who, along with Irish singer Mary Black, sat in with us for the television taping. Fran locked in with us from the moment he sat down behind his drum kit. He's a solid, hard-hitting rock drummer from the same school of legends as the late Irish drummer Dave Early and U2's distinguished drummer, Larry Mullen Jnr. Fran had been playing for years in some of Ireland's most innovative folk-rock bands, from Stockton's Wing and the Water Boys to Paul Brady. Fran joined our band during that television taping, and for the next ten years he and Pat McInerney became a wall of drum and percussion behind the Blue Moon Orchestra. He was also most of the drums for the sound track of Alan Parker's upbeat cult classic film about the Irish rock scene, *The Commitments.*

I heard our matriarch in the band, Lee Satterfield, playing rhythm guitar and singing backup for Jennifer Warnes in 1988. Lee is the single most talented woman I've met in music. She plays anything with strings, writes great songs, has the voice of a true angelic presence, and brings an incredible grace to our stage. Lee is originally from Colorado and learned a good deal of her stagecraft and art from watching artists from that area, like the Nitty Gritty Dirt Band. Her technical knowledge comes from her university studies at the Berklee College of Music in Boston. Lee is married to instrumentalist, composer, and symphony arranger John Moch, who has joined our band on many an occasion and played the pennywhistle on Stephen Foster's song "Hard Times Come Again No More." Lee's work on both volumes of *Other Voices* has been most stunning, from her mandolin to her vocals on Buddy Mondlock's "Comin' Down in the Rain" to her chameleonic third vocal with Lucinda Williams and me on "Wings of a Dove," the latter of which is barely heard until you take it away and the loss is heartbreaking. The song wouldn't be the same without her weaving our two vocals together. Overall, Lee is the most indefinable and brilliant talent in our band. Her whole heart goes into this music. If I could choose "the *Other Voice*" to be, it would be the voice of Lee Satterfield.

Ron de la Vega played cello and bass for a popular alternative folk band in Nashville called the Wine Skins. He began playing with us on a temporary basis, filling in for our bassist, Denny Bixby, who had left us to start his own band, Great Plains. Like Lee, Ron is classically trained and quietly brilliant at his work. He was with us for five years, but I was still introducing him as a special guest sitting in with the Blue Moon Orchestra from his own band, the Wine Skins. Our bandleader, James Hooker, finally pointed out to me that Ron obviously wasn't going back to his old band and that, after five years, I should be introducing him as a regular BMO band member. That was four years ago. Along with his cello and bass work, Ron is a wonderful harmony singer with a dynamic vocal range. His voice in this band is invaluable. Ron started his career as a session and symphony musician in Los Angeles before moving to Nashville with his wife, Karen, and their son, Ryan.

Doug Lancio is most commonly known as the juvenile of the BMO. He is the most versatile of players to have joined our band. He was well known around Nashville for his work in punk rock bands with Tom Littlefield and Jay Joyce in the Questionnaires and Bedlam. We call Doug our juvenile because he is the youngest band member and the newest, having joined us five years ago; yet he is not a juvenile in his playing. Doug is absolutely brilliant at his guitar work. Since joining our band he has tackled some odd instruments, including the resonator, and he shifts with ease from acoustic classical style to full-blown rock and roll on a Stratocastor to bluegrass

Nanci and her father,
Marlin Griffith
CARNEGIE HALL,
1993

photo by
Steve Sherman,
New York Times

left to right:
Doug Lancio, Nina Gerber,
James Hooker, Ron de la
Vega
NEW YORK, 1996

photo by Alan Messer

Lee Satterfield
NASHVILLE SESSION,
1997

photo by Alan Messer

*Nanci Griffith and Pete
Kennedy*
CAMBRIDGE FOLK
FESTIVAL, 1992

*photo from
Nanci Griffith's
personal collection*

Dobro sounds and blues on the resonator. He is one amazing player who has even started singing harmony with us onstage and in the recordings for our *Blue Roses from the Moons* anniversary album. Doug also has a great talent for producing, so we all suspect he'll one day join his friend Jay Joyce as one of music's most in-demand producers.

Honorary BMO members through the years have included James Hooker's fellow Amazing Rhythm Aces band mate, guitarist "Byrd" Burton. Byrd has played many tours with us and has recorded with us on four albums. Singer-songwriter-guitarist Frank Christian is possibly the most multi-style guitar genius in popular as well as classical music today, has worked on both volumes of *Other Voices,* and wrote the delightful song for volume one "Three Flights Up," which is a true joy to sing.

Nina Gerber, who was Kate Wolf's guitar player, began playing with me in 1984 on my tours of the West Coast and the Northeast. She is everyone's favorite guitarist in this band, honorary members included. Her contributions to this project have been incredible and her wizardry with Frank Christian and Doug Lancio on songs like "He Was a Friend of Mine" is a little trip to Carter Family heaven. Nina is from the San Francisco music scene and is today one of the most gifted producers in that area. She is welcome on our stage anytime anywhere.

I met guitarist Pete Kennedy during an *Austin City Limits* television taping with Mary Chapin Carpenter, the Indigo Girls, and Julie Gold. Pete is from the Washington, D.C., area, and had built quite a following there as a solo artist as well as having backed Kate Wolf and Carolyn Hester on numerous tours in the Northeast. Pete's a wonderful player who truly is like a gangster professor of music prowling about onstage in the guise of a folk guitarist. He worked two world tours with us, bringing his wife, Maura, along on the second one to sing harmony and to open the shows with Pete. Maura is a talented songwriter, and since those tours the two of them have become the engaging folk/rock songwriting duo the Kennedys. Both of them have contributed an enormous amount of love to *Other Voices,* including Pete's outstanding guitar work on Gordon Lightfoot's "Ten Degrees and Getting Colder," and Maura's vocals with Susan Cowsill and me on Sylvia Tyson's "You Were on My Mind."

Last but not least of our honorary members, a man I refer to as my evil twin at times and my brother of arms at others, is Tom Littlefield, who has been a co-writer, a friend, and a wonderful musical influence for me over the

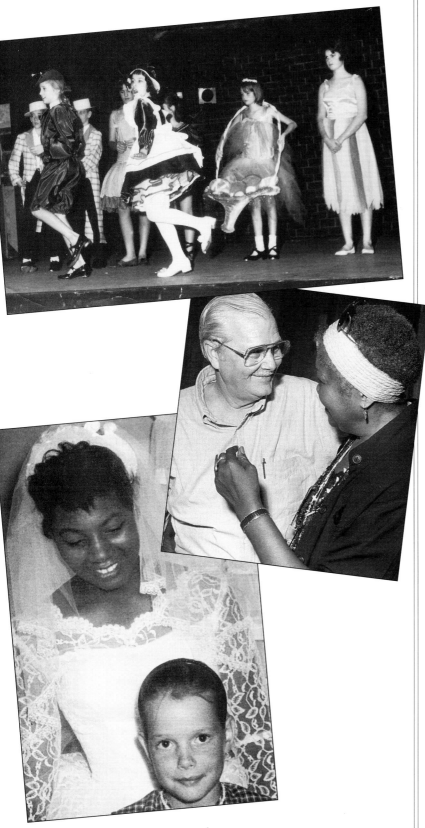

Rehearsals for Austin Civic Theatre's production of Gypsy. Nanci Griffith, age 9, is in the back row wearing a tutu and ankle socks.
1964

Marlin "Grif" Griffith with Odetta
NASHVILLE, 1993

Other Voices, Other Rooms

Nanci Griffith, age 8, and Marilyn Bush. Nanci was a flower girl for the wedding of Marilyn Bush. Marilyn lived in the Griffith family home while completing her studies and degree at the University of Texas at Austin. She is now a tenured professor at UCLA.

photos from Nanci Griffith's personal collection

past few years. Tom contributed vocally to the *Other Voices, Too* project, yet selflessly refused to take a vocal solo on songs like "Wasn't That a Mighty Storm." He preferred instead to remain in the background and take in the magic of these sessions in having so many of his heroes and contemporaries gathered together in the same studio for the common love of the musical heritage, especially in his love and admiration of Odetta. Tom is unique in his art of songwriting and guitar work as well as in his distinctive vocal style. He's considered a pioneer in his field for having crossed his initial passion for punk rock and roll with brilliant songwriting and for having moved beyond that stage to successfully achieve his goal as a full-time songwriter for other artists of all genres. It doesn't surprise me that Littlefield should be such a pioneer in music, it runs in his family: Tom is Woody Herman's grandson, which brings me full circle to my own childhood and my own mother's influence upon me.

Other Voices is like a musical rainbow that stretches from one horizon to the infinity and from one dream to another's heart. The Blue Moon Orchestra has been the pot of gold at either end.

A TRIP BACK TO BOUNTIFUL

Other Voices, Too: A Trip Back to Bountiful is my fifteenth album. I borrowed the latter part of this title from Horton Foote's Academy Award–winning film, *A Trip to Bountiful.* Geraldine Page won the Academy Award as Best Actress in 1985 for this film. It was her last film, and it's a classic American art treasure. It is the story of Carrie Watts, an elderly woman who journeys through Texas to return to her hometown of Bountiful. She believes the place of her roots to be the place to bring her life a joyous return to times of happiness and memories of fondness. Though she is a woman of little means of her own, she traverses this journey with the wealth of her childhood dreams for life's meaning, armed with her small pocketbook containing only her Social Security check. Her belief in the beauty of the soul of her home, Bountiful, is passed on to the strangers she encounters. (Along that journey to Bountiful, she changes those strangers' lives just with her passion for a time and a place and her propinquity for the destinies of her loved ones created there.)

Recording these *Other Voices* projects has truly been a trip to Bountiful for me as an artist. From the diverse influences of my parents' bohemian tastes in music to finding my own voice along this way, I have been fortunate to have been given the luxury to run totally amok artistically, allowing me to find this highway off the beaten path back to Bountiful. With the collaboration of my producers throughout my career I've been given the opportunity to explore music as diverse as my parents' hopes and dreams.

I've held close to my heart a note my father left on the dining table in my home in Austin in 1983, just a simple note that was left without solicitation for advice.

Who knows what prompts parents to write such things? We, as their children, are the lucky and fortunate ones indeed who receive them. I carry that note from my father with me wherever this road to Bountiful rolls. It's worn now . . . tattered around the edges just like his daughter, and with the support of my listeners and the knowledge of producers Tony Brown, Glynn Johns, Peter Van Hooke and Rod Argent, Jim Rooney, Peter Collins, and Don Gehman, the Blue Moon Orchestra and I have traveled through the unknown together without a single thought of becoming complacent or repeating ourselves. With each recording project I've been lent the invaluable opportunity to learn and to grow as a musician and as a writer.

Marci~ you must never become complacent with your art.

Love.
Dad~o

also ~ please don't take up smoking!

Through these fifteen albums, each so different in direction from the other, I've ended here in Bountiful, a reflection of my parents' differences and their life together.

My mother loves to hear me play rock and roll with the Crickets and she is over the moon that I have played with the Boston Pops and the Nashville Symphony and recorded with the string section of the London Philharmonic for my *Late Night Grande Hotel* album. She has enjoyed two trips to New York to see me perform at Carnegie Hall. She is like the character of Mama Rose in the play *Gypsy*, standing in the back of the theatre shouting, "Sing out, Louise! Sing out!" In retrospect, I myself am not too far from the character of Louise in *Gypsy*. I'm sure I'm a bit different as an artist than what my mother expected. She loathes contemporary country music.

She says it offends her ears. Though I adore traditional country music, my mother throws tantrums every time she goes into a music store and sees my records in the country section. She throws whatever's handy at the television anytime I'm introduced as "country singer Nanci Griffith."

She's over seventy still digging her jazz, watching MTV, and dressing weird. She's still quite beautiful, though her platinum hair is of a different source nowadays. She still entertains a group of friends one would consider a bit out of the ordinary even in these times. In fact, one of my mother's friends, whom she's been close to since high school, still can't get the approval of my grandmother, who is over ninety now and will never stop nagging my mother to stop hanging around with that particular friend. It is of my mother's character to remain a controversy throughout her life, just as her passion for her particular tastes in music, literature, art, and politics shall always be a delightful part of what she is in my own "Bountiful." It's a fragile balance of eccentricity and innocence that my mother has passed on to me as her daughter.

My father, true to the note he left me in 1983, is always a quiet supporter and a true champion. Though he's expressed great joy at attending my concerts all over the world, from the Royal Albert Hall in London to Carnegie Hall in New York to seeing the Nashville Ballet, with the Nashville Symphony, perform Paul Vasterling's contemporary ballet, *This Heart,* which is based on seven of my songs, I have seen his "proud father lights" shine the brightest, standing next to Odetta and Emmylou Harris singing these songs from *Other Voices.* My mother teases that it's because he knows the words to these songs better than the ones that I've written, yet I know that it is the tradition of passing on the music that makes him beam . . . that and getting to stand with his arm around Odetta and Emmylou.

From the dust-blown plains of my parents' West Texas along this highway so rich in treasures, I hope these collections of songs bring to my listeners a memorable and joyous trip with the true companionship of all of these unique and colorful singers, writers, and musicians to their own Bountiful and back again.

I have certainly been blessed to have traveled this distance of fifteen very different and eclectic record projects with the ears of my listeners throughout these years. Just as my parents have chosen favorites of my records according to their own particular passions, so have my audiences, and I have long given up guessing which record makes a particular person's day . . . selfishly, as an artist, each record had to make my day with my music to make it to print. Yet the one thing I have found that both my audiences and my parents together share is the love of the *Other Voices* recordings. It's perhaps a common simplicity. A turn of a heart to a time in one's life. It's a warm place to be . . . for me, like the small child curled up on a hardwood floor of a Sunday evening watching *Walt Disney's Wonderful World of Color* in 1961 when the television show breaks to a commercial and it's a Kodak ad full of color you can't really see because your TV's black and white, yet you feel that color of image with the visions of home movies and the music of a song, "Turn Around," by Harry Belafonte and Malvina Reynolds. It's Carolyn Hester's voice you're hearing singing that song, and you don't know or care about any of that when you're that child so warm and intrigued . . . it's just the song, the image, and the clarity of paving a highway to your own sound track in your own "Bountiful" in your own time and sense of place.

p r e l u d e

It's not often that one sees the spirit captured in a moment that will probably echo throughout time—the spirit of music, the spirit of art as an emotional imperative, and the spirit of a singer acting as a conduit for everything that is transcendent and true. However, all of these fluencies are clearly evident in Gerry O'Leary's photograph, which adorns the back cover of this book. It was taken during the recording sessions for *Other Voices, Too* while Nanci Griffith was listening to the playback of Stephen Foster's "Hard Times Come Again No More." The sense of wonder was still there in her voice nearly half a year later when I asked her if she could recall precisely what she was feeling at the moment when O'Leary's camera clicked.

"I have this old Saint Christopher medal that was given to me by my boyfriend when I was twelve, and when I'm really hopeful or really intense, it always ends up in my hand," Nanci said, sitting cross-legged on the floor of her home in Tennessee. But you can see from that picture of Jim Rooney and me that we are so happy with what we're hearing. When

Nanci Griffith
1 9 8 4

photo by
David Gahr

51

Dolores Keane's voice kicked in on 'Hard Times Come Again No More,' she was that 'pale sorrowed maiden.' She *is* the soul of Ireland. You can hear her crying. And everyone at the session was crying. It was a powerful moment. Also, you have Lucy Kaplansky coming in, doing the high part, and that adds another layer of ethereal beauty. As did the fact that Nollaig Casey and Mary Custy were reading and playing from Stephen Foster's original charts, which really brought the whole thing back to basics, back home, in every sense. We felt like we had brought Stephen Foster back to his ancestral home of Ireland. It was that magical."

Listening to Nanci Griffith speak on that day when we began work on this book, I couldn't help but think of the afternoon four years earlier when she and I had first discussed *Other Voices, Other Rooms*. I had interviewed her before, but—fittingly, perhaps—this was the first time I realized that Nanci really does see herself as a human tuning fork, a form of musical instrument through which other voices, other spirits, flow and—hopefully—take flight. In other words, she sees herself as a folksinger in the purest sense, a conduit for all that is common but also uncommonly rare. *Other Voices,* was, of course, her first album of material composed exclusively by other songwriters and, more specifically, by the artists who had inspired Nanci Griffith to turn to music as a child and who, as she said, "gave me roots." Nowhere was this more apparent than during the recording of Townes Van Zandt's "Tecumseh Valley," which also brought tears not only to Nanci's eyes but also to Arlo Guthrie's, because both felt, she says, "reconnected, so acutely, with where we come from, who we are, through the character in that song."

This acute sense of being almost forcibly hauled back to face who we are —in essence—and where we come from, Nanci hopes, will be the public response to *Other Voices,* both the albums and this book. Indeed, her core belief in the transformative power of music is central to Nanci's perception of the project, not just in terms of transporting the soul back to its original state of grace but even of calling a soul back from beyond the grave. The latter is an experience Nanci recalls from the recording session that produced Kate Wolf's "Across the Great Divide" for the first album.

"Kate was the inspiration for my writing my own song, 'Ford Econoline,' which was, in part, about her life," Nanci explains. "And Kate was a great writer, but unfortunately she died at the time she was beginning to get exposure. So there really was the same level of emotion in the studio

Joe Jackson and Nineyear
Wooldridge, Nanci's tour
and production manager
SUMMER 1997

photo by Alan Messer

front row:
Pam Rose, Mary Ann
Kennedy, Dave Mallet,
Nanci Griffith, Holly
Tashian, Emily Saliers,
John Prine
second row:
John Gorka, Leo Kotke, Amy
Ray, Odetta, Barry Tashian
back row:
Mark Miller, Roy
Huskey Jr., Jim
Rooney, Marlin
"Griff" Griffith,
James Hooker
NASHVILLE
1993

"Wimoweh"

photo by
Beth Gwinn

when Emmylou Harris and I were recording 'Across the Great Divide' as there was when Arlo and I did 'Tecumseh Valley.' I don't want to sound over-romantic, but Kate's song title is apt. She had a very identifiable voice, and during the recording session every time I sang the song I could hear her voice again. Emmylou said the same thing. We both really couldn't help but sing in Kate's voice rather than our own."

Asked if she was really convinced that a song could carry the soul of a person across the great divide between death and life and that Wolf was present in spirit in that studio, Nanci Griffith is categoric in her reply. "I definitely believe so," she says. "We all felt that's what was echoing in the studio, and I hope listeners can feel the peacefulness and the beauty of Kate Wolf when they hear her music."

Other Voices, Other Rooms also can be seen as a manifestation of Nanci Griffith's own attempt to cross that great divide between life and death, not just in terms of folksingers who have been silenced but also in terms of songs that have been consigned to a similar fate and all the personal and social histories that are lost as a result of this process and which would remain lost if the market-driven and less than socially self-conscious music industry had its way. Moving against such forces is another motivating factor behind Nanci's involvement in the project. In fact, when we first discussed the album she poured considerable scorn on the stereotypical "stupid record executive with a cigar in his mouth who sat back all those years ago and decided that folk music wasn't 'commercial' and didn't deserve to be played on the radio." She also acerbically noted that folk is the "*f*-word" as far as the record industry is concerned. She pointed out that you don't have to be a Luddite to know that the day the development of music is dictated purely by marketing strategies will be the day the music dies—at least as a form of human expression. Happily, by way of contrast, you have recordings like "Wimoweh," the closing track on her first *Other Voices, Other Rooms* collection, which says it all, as far as Nanci Griffith is concerned, because it features three generations of folksingers, from Odetta to the Indigo Girls.

"To see Odetta leading all these people into the fold by saying, 'Come on in, let's do this together,' was another wonderful moment for me," she recalls. "I would love it if people hear what she is saying, in the widest sense, and go back through these albums to the world of folk music, which really is the most neglected roots music in America."

Nanci Griffith ain't joking. She really does believe that folksingers like Odetta, Leadbelly, Mance Lipscomb, and Woody Guthrie "defined America every bit as much as Abraham Lincoln, Henry Ford, and Martin Luther King Jr." Given such a claim, it should come as no surprise to learn that Nanci Griffith took the title for this entire project from a novel by Truman Capote, who certainly brought a new visionary sensibility to American literature when he published his first novel, *Other Voices, Other Rooms,* which Nanci describes as "a deeply moving and evocative book about returning home." Nevertheless, Nanci Griffith has listened to, and written, enough folk songs to realize that the concept of returning home is often little more than a romantic illusion. She knows, in her own soul, that for so many of us the song itself is the only "home" we are ever likely to know again.

Either way, packing our bags for such a journey certainly seems like a sensible thing to do right now, particularly as we prepare for a new millennium and try to decide what we should take with us and what we should leave behind, if only in order to determine who we were, who we are, and who we want to become. And if these albums or this book can place a single stepping-stone on that path for even one person, then Nanci Griffith and I will have realized our objectives.

And—oh, yes—you've probably noted by now that, for some strange reason, Nanci Griffith's music seems to make people cry or at least feel emotions that are normally repressed. But not this boy. The light liquid lines tracing their way down my cheek the first time I heard "Hard Times Come Again No More" were purely a result of the water leaking from the roof in Nanci's guesthouse. Then again, maybe it was that mighty storm. In my heart. In all our hearts. That, to me, is the healing power of folk music. And that's why I am immensely proud to be working with Nanci Griffith on this book.

—Joe Jackson, Dublin, February 1998

1

nanci griffith:
folksinger

Other Voices, Other Rooms has its origins in the intertwining of two voices in one very specific room. And as in their recording of "Across the Great Divide," those two voices belong to Nanci Griffith and Emmylou Harris, who were, Nanci recalls, "just sitting around talking on New Year's Eve in 1992" about their mutual love of folk music. The conversation turned to the "beauty and clarity" of Kate Wolf's music, in particular.

"We spoke of both the sadness in her passing and the lack of new voices singing Kate's songs. Emmy said songs need new voices to sing them in places they've never been sung in order to stay alive," Nanci wrote in her sleeve notes to *Other Voices, Other Rooms,* identifying that night as the point at which the album was conceived. Elsewhere, however, Nanci claimed that the idea for the album had been gestating for at least "ten, twenty years" and that she now realizes that the "true seeds" of the project were probably planted way back in her childhood.

"I always had a respect for passing on the music, because my father always taught me that you should," she says reflectively. "And I first learned of folk music from my father. So that tradition was instilled in me, and so was respect for the tradition he carried forward by being a barbershop quartet singer. But folk music is his love as well. And that love includes the desire to preserve this music as a form of communal expression and as a narrative of its times, a kind of literature. My grandfather also looked on music as something that should be shared, enjoyed, passed on from one generation to another. And my mother was a big jazz buff, so the side of me that cherishes Nat 'King' Cole, big band stuff, Count Basie, and so on comes more from that side of the family. And let's not forget that jazz has the same roots as folk music. Composers like Basie and Duke Ellington are *great* American artists, as are the best rap artists. It's all folk culture, as far as I'm concerned, and a lot of my beliefs in this area come straight from my family."

Nanci has always acknowledged that when she was growing up in Texas during the early 1960s, folk music was her first love. Whenever she focuses on those days Nanci invariably and joyfully recalls that the voice of Carolyn Hester, spiraling forth from a transistor radio, gave her "wings to fly and a place to be while the radio was dominated by rock and roll." But this doesn't mean that the young Nanci Griffith was infected with the kind of snobbery that, in those days, made too many so-called folk purists despise rock music. On the contrary, she "adored" rockers like the Everly Brothers and readily embraces the revisionist notion that the early rockabilly singers from Texas, like Buddy Holly and the Crickets—and their role models, Elvis Presley, Carl Perkins, and Johnny Cash in Memphis—were also great original American folk artists.

"It's like Jim Rooney says. People like Buddy, Sonny Curtis, J.I., Joe B., and Glen D. Hardin all started out listening to Bill Monroe and Hank Williams." She happily elaborates, naming Holly's band, the Crickets. "They were very into folk music. Woody Guthrie, that was their thing. J.I. has said that the first time they went to England they heard Lonnie Donegan and realized that his version of 'Rock Island Line' was a folk song turned into skiffle. The Crickets were inspired by that, because they were already into what they called rock and roll, or rockabilly, which is much the same as what the British called skiffle. The Crickets realized it was all the same, drawing on Monroe, Guthrie, Ledbetter [Leadbelly], whoever. All of this was happening around the same time, and later, of course, it led to the folk boom of the late fifties and early sixties, which also became a big part of my life."

Given that folk and rockabilly were two of her original influences, Nanci Griffith agrees, to a degree, with the folkabilly tag once slapped on her music by *Rolling Stone.* Nevertheless, when it comes to discussing early rock and roll, why is it that Nanci always sings the praises of, say, Buddy Holly rather than Elvis?

"It wasn't that we thought Buddy was better than Elvis, Gene Vincent, or whoever, it was more that his was a voice we *understood.* I myself certainly liked Buddy's music and didn't care too much for Elvis, but maybe that was simply because I just didn't understand him, whereas when it came to Buddy Holly there was something about his music that, for a child my age, got me greatly interested in the songs of Buddy and Sonny Curtis, right from the beginning. And because of my folk base I'd always check out the songwriters, which I guess a lot of pop fans didn't do at the time. Then again I also had this great love of the voice. The Everly Brothers really were the first singers I heard on the radio who made me hide under the sheets and long to listen to them late at night. Their vocal quality was so pure and has never been matched. The difference between them and their countless imitators is like the difference between a synthesizer and an orchestra. A synthesizer is great and useful, but when you walk into a room and you hear a real orchestra, there's something magical, mystical, about the sound of wood— real instruments. It's the same with regard to the sound of the Everly Brothers. Don Everly does lead, but Phil is the genius when it comes to harmonizing. And that's an area that doesn't always receive the praise it deserves, because people focus too much on the voice out front."

To successive generations of folk fans Woody Guthrie was the sole voice out front in every sense. He was also the singer that Nanci Griffith claims she first heard "in the womb" because her father was a "Guthrie freak." But there were other seminal influences from the field of folk music.

"I was very impressed when Bob Dylan came along, but my sister was more into Dylan," Nanci recalls. "I had my own heroes—John Stewart, for example. And I always loved Harlan Howard's songs because although I didn't listen much to country radio, occasionally Buck Owens would break through onto pop radio with a Harlan Howard song. That, to me, was just magic. Among the women, of course, there was Loretta Lynn, whom I still adore and who definitely was a role model. Then, as I've said so often, there was Carolyn Hester, who was not only a wonderful singer and writer but, unlike Baez, she had rhythm! But then Carolyn had been good friends with Buddy Holly and did some of her records with Sonny Curtis out in New Mexico. For her first Columbia album she also brought Bob Dylan in to play harmonica. So she had those rock leanings. And they've rereleased her old albums with an advertisement saying, 'If you've heard Nanci Griffith, you've heard Carolyn Hester.' It's true, because our voices are very similar, and when I was a child, that was what I wanted to sound like." Even so, Nanci stresses yet again that she was no folk snob. She did not dismiss all "commercial" popular music.

"I never saw it that way because pop, to me, at the time, was Dylan, who, when I was young, was such a massive star," she reflects. "And my sister really was such a big fan of his. *That* was popular music, because 'Like a Rolling Stone' was being played on the radio every ten minutes, and it was six minutes long and folk music, without a doubt, as far as I was concerned. But my parents didn't like Dylan, to begin with. My dad would say, 'If you're going to listen to this, go to the source,' so he would pass on his Woody Guthrie records to me, as more 'authentic.' He'd say, 'This is what Bob Dylan is,' but I don't think he was paying full attention to Dylan, so that was evidence, right there, of folk music snobbery. He probably never sat down and analyzed the fact that Guthrie himself had taken all these old Leadbelly melodies and put new words to them, as in 'Rambling Round' is 'Good Night, Irene,' and so on. They're all intermixed, but my dad never realized that."

Clearly, *Other Voices, Other Rooms* also has its origins in Nanci Griffith's father telling her to go back to the source. In that album's sleeve notes she says, "I harbor great hopes that those who hear these songs for the first time, and discover a genre of music they'd like to hear more of, will go out to the record store and search through the bins to find the original works of these artists and writers." Isn't this, again, an example of Nanci carrying on a folk tradition that, in her case, was also a family tradition?

"Yes, I guess it is." She nods, smiling. "And Dad would tell me to go back to people like Dave Van Ronk. And the Weavers in particular, who were played nonstop in our house. We'd be woken up at six o'clock in the morning hearing the Weavers on these little speakers we had in every room, from the record player, when hi-fi systems first came on the market. Or we'd wake up to Odetta singing 'Kumbaya,' and then we'd walk out into the hallway and she'd follow us! So how on earth could you not end up singing those songs? And Dad'd play Woody Guthrie's children's album, so we grew up listening to Woody singing 'Take Me Riding in the Car,' all that stuff."

Growing up in the Griffith household, it obviously also was pretty impossible to avoid picking up a guitar or playing piano. "Everybody was expected to play something. My brother played horns, and he and my sister were very good on piano," Nanci remembers. "But I just couldn't learn piano because of my dyslexia. . . . I needed to be doing something where I couldn't watch my hands, where I could just let the hands do, artistically, what they need to be doing. So guitar was natural. My sister had bought one, and she was in a folk trio, and I would sneak into her room and play her guitar. My dad got me a Woody Guthrie songbook, a Burl Ives songbook, all kinds of things like that."

Although turning to the guitar and music may have been natural for Nanci Griffith, her original ambition was to be a writer. In the cover photo of her album *The Last of the True Believers,* Nanci is pressing to her chest a copy of *The Kindness of Strangers* by Donald Spoto, giving the strongest possible clue to her own psycho-literary base. On the back of the same album she is seen clasping a novel by Larry McMurtry.

"Literature in general influenced me so heavily because I was not an outgoing child," she explains. "It also gave me the desire to be a writer because it did become that magical place for me to go. As soon as I learned how to read, at just over four years old, reading became my companion. My grandmother taught me—though, again, I had a hard time with reading, as I did with school, because of my dyslexia. But the book I first really hooked into was *Grimms' Fairy Tales.* Then, later, Truman Capote, Tennessee Williams, Carson McCullers, and Eudora Welty, in particular. She really got me into southern literature in that she wrote about rebellious adolescents and endowed those characters with a wonderful sense of themselves. So she helped me through adolescence. And what young woman hasn't read Tennessee Williams and fallen madly in love with him? When I was in high school I had an English teacher who told me that Tennessee was a homosexual, and it broke my heart because my cousin Libby and I used to go past his estate in New Orleans, and I'd hang by the gates waiting for him to come out—not knowing Tennessee Williams didn't actually live there. Though maybe 'come out' is the wrong phrase! But, seriously, as a child, these writers were like pop stars to me, and like Eudora Welty, Williams wrote about people who felt dislocated, disenfranchised, and were misfits, and that's what I loved about him. Yet what was really fascinating was that Tennessee Williams could take someone who was a misfit in society and give them a sense of normalcy. And as for Larry McMurtry, he moved me so much because he too gave me a sense of place, though, in his case, more in a geographic sense. He wrote about Texas in modern times, which was all I understood. I never understood Texas as being full of cowboys with boots and hats, because it isn't."

Nanci Griffith also never understood Texas as being "full of" anything. She wholeheartedly agrees with Roy Orbison who once said that, growing up in Texas, there was "absolutely nothing to look at" and that made being lonely almost a "normal" state of mind, or heart. And this, Nanci claims, was the impulse behind her need to "conjure alternative realities" in literature and music. Nanci's own personal sense of separateness, however, was accentuated by the fact that her parents divorced when she was a child. Did this lead to her further absorbing the shared worldview of Williams and D. H. Lawrence, both of whom believed that the natural state for men and women was to be at war with each other? "Not in an absolute sense," she says, pondering the question. "I wouldn't have perceived the sexes *only* as continually battling each other," she says. "But I would say that the biggest creative head-on clashes I've had have been with men who were heavily influenced by Ernest Hemingway, because his view was so like [that of] Lawrence—this idea that women were definitely not equal to men, that they were no intellectual match for them whatsoever. I would have gotten the exact opposite view of women from my reading as a child and adolescent, particularly from Williams, who presented magnificent portraits of women in his work."

All this living soul-deep in literature during Nanci Griffith's formative years also later led to what she glowingly describes as "that wonderful moment when the act of reading became a sense of believing that I, too, could become a writer." As in a writer of songs. "I was such a primitive guitar player that it became easier to write something of my own and go in and play it for my dad or brother or sister," she explains. "I started doing that when I was six, seven."

But why did Nanci turn to writing songs rather than writing books?

"Because it was such an immediate thing and I haven't got a real long attention span," she responds, laughing. "But seriously, I think I was such an avid listener, as well as loving to play, that I never really thought about it, so there was no road to Damascus. I just evolved into a performer, into recording. The whole thing really did start with me seeing music as a form of self-expression, just like the poetry I wrote in high school. Yet even those poems read more like lyrics than poetry. And I have used fragments of those poems in my songs, poems that were written way back in my teens."

More to the point, in terms of the style of self-expression that defines Nanci Griffith and her art, she also taps into feelings that have been floating around since those days, feelings that are often unresolved until she sets them down in song. As in "So Long Ago" from her 1988 album *Little Love Affairs.* This lyric, she believes, marks the beginning of her loss of emotional innocence.

"That song was a way for me to exorcise a ghost of my own, because I had a boyfriend from the age of twelve to seventeen, and he was killed in a motorcycle accident," she recalls. "And Eric Taylor, who later became my husband and is now a psychologist and dear friend, always said, 'You really must exorcise that someday. Why don't you try writing about it?' That's basically what I did with 'So Long Ago,' and it really did help me. For example, as I was getting older, this person still remained a naive seventeen-year-old in my mind, and I found that hard to deal with."

As she relates this tale in an almost painfully self-conscious manner, one realizes that Nanci Griffith, like her idol and mentor, Townes Van Zandt, is one of those artists blessed with the ability to translate personal pain into music that is truly universal.

"That phone call telling us Townes had died was a phone call all of us who knew him had been expecting for twenty years, though the circumstances were very unexpected," she says. "But we were all very happy that he was at home, with his family. Yet he'd been writing about death for years. As in 'Tell my friends to mourn me none' or 'If I had no place to fall,' all that. But when it comes to what, yes, some would see as his self-destructive lifestyle—his need to sacrifice everything for art—the beauty of Townes, and the hallmark of his work, is that he had the courage as a writer to go places. Physically. He had to physically be there and feel it so that the rest of us wouldn't have to. But then, Townes couldn't have done it any other way. And he is such a brilliant writer that I think his songs will still be around in another hundred years, which, to me, does make it all worthwhile. He was just an incredible poet-writer who internalized everything. Everything went through him."

That said, isn't it potentially lethal to send out to young songwriters, in particular, the coded message that you have to travel physically into the

*Carolyn Hester at
Emmajoe's*
SEPTEMBER 1982

*photo by Wayne
Miller*

Jim Rooney
DUBLIN, 1997

*photo by
Gerry O'Leary*

*photo from
Nanci Griffith's
personal collection*

bowels of every possible human experience before your songs can breathe for other people or live beyond time?

"I think it is a dangerous message to send out, yes, but it depends on what type of writer you are." In the light, or rather shade, of these revelations one begins to understand why Nanci's own style of folk song—from the earliest, such as "Song for Remembered Heroes," through "Fields of Summer," right up to many of the tracks on *Blue Roses from the Moons*—depicts the singer as a dark-hearted, wounded romantic. Is *that* how Nanci Griffith perceives herself?

"Well, I've always had a soft spot for the wounded artist, people who are off the beaten track a little," she says, smiling. "And that's why I always found artists like Townes Van Zandt and Tom Waits so inspiring. Because Tom, in particular, can create such enormous, colorful fiction out of that wounded romanticism. And that description does fit me, in the widest sense. I am very eccentric, in ways."

Nanci Griffith also claims that her own form of "wounded romanticism" is very much rooted in emotional deprivation, though she also has, she says, "lived in dire poverty" on many occasions.

"You can't erase that memory," she explains. "But then, surely the real point is that the kind of poverty which fires many singers and artists, in general, is *emotional* poverty rather than any other form of deprivation. You can be a multimillionaire and still sing like a hollow shell. That, to me, is not that far removed from the pain brought on by poverty. Equally, people who live on modest means can still feel complete, if they are loved. And, as I say, I've known both sides of life. But above and beyond all this, I really am a writer who writes about emotional poverty more than anything else. And that, to me, *is* the common experience. It's the same in terms of many of the songs I chose to record for *Other Voices, Other Rooms*. On the first volume there is that song 'Are You Tired of Me, Darling' The two men who wrote that were writing about emotional poverty in 1877. Shakespeare also wrote about emotional longing. That's been a feature of art, throughout time."

As has spiritual poverty, which some social commentators suggest is a defining feature of art, if not life, in the twentieth century. Specifically in terms of the so-called death of God and the increasing secularization of society. Some people, it's claimed, sublimate this longing into a desire for a soul mate or into a belief in art, music, even a belief in pop stars. Does Nanci herself agree, or does she see all this as overanalysis taken to a ludicrous degree?

"I see it all in those terms," she says. "My religious base is Catholic, yet I've gone on to study so many religions, as an avid reader, and find that this searching aspect in my character has now left me very spiritually centered. Not in the sense that I believe in one God. There are so many things to learn from Mohammed, from Buddha. And even with Catholicism . . . , Christianity, though you may question many of its tenets, there also is so much we can learn from, say, the writing of the saints. As in Saint Teresa of Avila, who also wrote chants and was, of course, the inspiration for the song of the same name on my *Blue Roses* album. And as a result of studying all the common factors between religions, I do, for example, really believe that when I sing that song about Saint Teresa of Avila it helps bring back the spirit of a friend of mine who committed suicide a few years ago. It's concepts like that that I tap into for inspiration now, rather than turning to any one notion of God. And in a sense this also obviously is evidence of the fact that, like so many people this century, I happen to believe in art above everything else—in my case, music."

Indeed, when asked if a sense of spiritual calm is basically what Nanci Griffith would want her music to bring to listeners, she shivers and says, "Oh, God, if only." She draws back, however, when told that Dion DiMucci once told this writer that, without knowing exactly whose voice he was hearing on the radio, he identified immediately the "spiritual power" in Nanci Griffith's music. Is this what Nanci sees as sitting at the heart of her work?

"I can't really say what's at the core of my work. But if people like Dion hear that, I couldn't be happier."

Nevertheless, despite her reticence in relation to this subject, for many of Nanci's fans the spiritual-emotional power in her voice is a defining feature of her appeal. Similarly, it could be argued that the nameless hunger in Nanci's own soul dictates not just the nature of the songs she writes but also the songs she chooses as representative of folk culture on both *Other Voices* albums. After all, many of these folktales are variations on the theme of a wanderer who is less Dion than Schubert, a creature longing to return home, or aching deep down because of an inability to do so. Also central to both albums is, as I suggested earlier, this sense that the song itself becomes the home. Likewise, the act of singing. Is that how Nanci feels? When she sings, and connects with an audience, is that really as close to a feeling of home as she believes she will ever know?

"I think all that is true, definitely," she reflects, having fallen silent for a few moments and taken one more sip from her glass of wine. "The song *is* the home, that place to be, that center," she says almost sadly. "And what you say about the singing and performing really is true, in the sense that I feel I am at my purest when I connect with an audience. For a lot of people the only point we feel we connect is at moments like that. So that, too, is God, I guess. It's the same thing when it comes to writing songs. Sometimes I really do feel that the songs aren't mine, that they belong to someone else or are just passing by, and I reach out and grab them because I have good timing. Or because I'm suddenly in touch with some force out there, whatever that force may be." Nanci admits that at times like this her abiding sense of isolation evaporates, as it does for many performers, though it rolls back in right after the song ends.

"In a way it does, yes," she reflects. "I've had times, even before Townes Van Zandt died, when I would finish 'Tecumseh Valley' [Townes's song performed by Nanci and Arlo Guthrie on *Other Voices, Other Rooms*], and there would have to be some other thing for me to do on the stage immediately, because I couldn't deal with the intensity of the sense of loneliness as I sang about the character of Caroline. It was too much. Because she is someone who just tried so hard to find something in life, but still couldn't get up on her feet. That hurts so bad. Townes just takes you so far into this woman that it hurts that deeply, and when the song is over, I have to go and mess around with James Hooker and his keyboards, do anything, just to have somewhere else to go, to rest, to pull myself back together. I can't go straight into another piece of music because I am feeling Caroline's loneliness too intrinsically. The sense of her hurt does not leave me. And since, as I said on many occasions, I feel as if I could have been Caroline, I guess it's my own pain I'm feeling, too."

What does Nanci mean? That she could have been broken by life, like the subject in the Van Zandt song?

"Yeah, but then I feel that everyone has that potential to fail," she suggests. "And everyone has the potential to bring on a chain of events that lead to a failure that is not their own, as in her case. . . . But the thing about that song is that, through making that journey, Caroline became a guardian angel for me, a presence that will forever ensure that I never fall that low. Because I never forget I could have been her. That song kept me from being her. I always had this concept within myself that I cannot fail and I cannot fall because there is no place to fall. The fall is death. And I always did believe that if I fall, there is no one to pick me up. So, from that song, I've always been given that strength by Townes Van Zandt. But I really relate to his character of Caroline because I left home at sixteen, and I knew once I closed the door I could never go back."

Surely believing that "the fall is death" is needlessly severe? If not on others then on oneself? Doesn't Nanci ever long to fold into the feeling of "God, let me fall, let me collapse, let someone else come and help me out of this"? Or similar feelings?

"No. I don't ever yield to such feelings," she states categorically. "Because I've seen too many people fall and not get back up. Maybe if I had come from a different background, a more stable environment, maybe I would feel it's okay to fall, but now I don't." Such feelings often can be a consequence of the fragmentation of one's family, even if, as in Nanci's case, the parents do stay close, as she earlier suggested. But after her folks' marriage fell apart, didn't Nanci ever feel, for example, "Oh, I can call my dad"? "No. I felt I could call him as a friend, but my father didn't understand responsibility until I was on my own. And since he discovered what that is, he's been a great father," she explains. "But my parents were not great caregivers. They were very self-absorbed, which was probably part of the beatnik ethos. As with hippies, part of that whole thing was that people learned to care about social concerns and issues but not how to care for each other as individuals. I have a lot of friends like that, and we joke about how the last word they remember before they go to sleep is their own last name! That's all they say before they go to sleep!"

Nevertheless, despite these claims of almost total independence, Nanci Griffith obviously doesn't stop herself from falling—in love. However, like another of her favorite authors, Erich Fromm, she questions the use of the word "falling" in relation to love, believing that "rising," not "falling," should be the motion initiated as a result of love. "You have to grow in order to remain together," she suggests. "You have to get past the state of being in love and move into the state of mutual respect and recognizing each other's needs, even if those needs take you in opposite directions. And that is what I've always believed."

All this talk could, of course, indicate that a person has way too romantic a view of life and is far too idealistic when it comes to love. Mightn't this be true of Nanci Griffith? "Probably, yes!" she replies, laughing. "And John Stewart calls me the Garbo of the music industry because I write songs about relationships and about marriages, yet he's never seen me involved with anyone. In that sense I do have a very romantic view of love, but I also write something like 'It's Too Late,' which is a very realistic view of the tensions that are inevitable in a relationship. So I do know that life can't *always* be romantic. But I do still truly believe in love. I am a true believer in that sense, though not, I hope, one of the last."

Would Nanci ever fear that if she does finally center herself in a relationship rather than in her music, the hunger will cease and the songs fade to silence or, at best, be reduced to relatively vacuous mush?

"If I was only an introspective songwriter, rather than someone who also writes journalistic works, that might be the case," she responds, bringing into the sharpest possible focus the fact that, despite many claims to the contrary, Nanci Griffith is not simply a product of the "me" generation of singer-songwriters but also a master of the art of telling narrative tales. "Then again, you can travel back to other heartaches, some of which never go away. I'm still drawing on emotional experiences from at least ten, twenty years ago in my latest work. So in that sense a songwriter can live in a form of emotional flux, caught somewhere between the past and the present."

Shifting the conversation from a discussion of the more personal and confessional nature of her songs to their broader political implications, Nanci rejects the notion that her absorption of gothic romances has led to a passive acceptance of the role of women as victims.

"Well, I myself have always been strong-willed and incapable of being the victim of anyone," she says quite forcefully. "And any of my characters—say, the character in 'Ford Econoline' or the character in 'Listen to the Radio'—are nobody's victims. They were victims for a brief moment in their lives, and then they said 'Get off my bumper, I'm out of here,' which is also very much me. And the character in 'Ford Econoline' is part Kate Wolf, who was hardly a victim. It's also inspired by Rosalie Sorrels, about whom one could say the same thing. But then, this is basically the image of strong women that comes across in folk music. Going back to Maybelle and Sarah in the Carter Family. They always sang about strong women, though those weren't their own songs. Same with Loretta Lynn, who was a real role model for me. Those were songs she'd written, and that was my ideal of what a woman was. Not a victim at all."

Nevertheless, Irish folksinger Maura O'Connell has claimed that whenever she heard the Clancy Brothers sing the refrain "Fine girl you are," she certainly didn't feel fine. On the contrary, she concluded that the representation of women in folk music is normally ridiculously one-dimensional and reductive.

"That's not the perspective I took from folk music," counters Nanci, a little surprised by the statement, "either in terms of my own family background or the folk music I was listening to since I was a child. And I've never noticed my audiences being sexist. Men have always been very respectful to me—in clubs, for example. I've never really had any problems along those lines. And, as I say, even in terms of country music, it was women like Loretta Lynn I was drawn to, and women are never reduced to less than something complex, complete, in her songs."

But surely the same isn't true of folk music in general, where, for example, women could hardly be said to be presented as complete in a sexual sense. One could even suggest that women in folk music, from the 1960s onward, were desexualized to a great degree, as is also true of many of the songs written by Nanci herself, at least in the sense that her music rarely celebrates physical love, pure and simple—or not so pure.

"I think there is more spiritual love celebrated in my work than physical, that's for sure, but that has got nothing to do with my equating sex with guilt. I never was that way inclined!" she says, laughing. "But the denial of sexuality is a factor in folk music, in a lot of ways. As in the fact that Joan Baez always went onstage barefoot and always stood perfectly still, not drawing any attention to her body. That, I think, was a way of not drawing attention to woman as a sexualized being in the way, say, that Elvis did, in terms of men in rock and roll—and blues singers and at least some folk artists, though blues wins this one by a mile, particularly in terms of female blues singers. But a folksinger like Elizabeth Cotten wrote some very assertive songs, in a sexual sense! She definitely rides that fine line between 'Is this folk or is it blues?' But, no, sex is not a big factor in the songs I've written or the songs I include on the *Other Voices* albums. Though, on the first, the song 'Are You Tired of Me, Darling' does focus on a woman who is really worried about her sexuality, because it appears her husband has lost passion for her."

Shifting from the subject of sexual politics to politics proper, Nanci claims that her parents always were politically active and that their sense of social responsibility at this level was sharpened by the music they loved.

"My mother was a very left-wing Democrat, though my father was a bit more moderate," she says. "But my grandparents were also very involved in the civil rights movement. Whenever Martin Luther King Jr. was on the radio or television, everything came to a stop. And even though I was very young I knew who Malcolm X was. It was very much part of our household. You were taught to pay attention and to fight for the rights of others. And the music we grew up with was an echo of that concern, probably partly shaped that consciousness, which is the great thing about folk music. And I'm sure that the music my parents and my grandparents chose reflected their political idealism. I also see myself as very much part of their lineage. I think it is important that every generation is captured and crystallized in songs, stories, whatever. Preserving the history of each generation of humankind is like creation to me. There is the urge to continue that. And the way I do it is through music. I certainly try to bring real live people into my music and champion regular people, regular folks."

What is Nanci's response to the claim that the more traditional forms of folk music have been replaced by rap and hip-hop, and deserve to be, because folk somehow ceased to reflect the concerns of the people en masse and centered more on the quest for personal fulfillment?

"Rap and gangsta music is folk music as it reflects an uncensored personal perspective of a particular time and social culture. Folk music has always done that," she responds. "You've always had two very distinctive and separate types of writers in folk music. Kate Wolf wrote of internal life, spiritual growth, and Guy Clark writes character studies, which are a reflection of their times and the social climate. Those writers [like Clark] are more like Guthrie, journalists-in-song, and that's the line that has been extended by rap and hip-hop. Those now are the musical voices of discontent. And what you might call the more traditional form of folk still has its radical voices in people like Billy Bragg and Butch Hancock."

Maybe so. But aren't these the exceptions that prove that folksingers have long since given up their battle for either labor rights, à la Guthrie, or civil rights, in the style of folksingers from the early sixties, like Pete Seeger? Hasn't folk music been co-opted in much the same sense that folkies always said was true of pop and rock?

"I don't see things that way," says Nanci. "I don't think that all folksingers are just self-concerned. I can't really speak for where other songwriters are coming from, but I do know that, as a writer myself, I'm still touching on subjects that are controversial and which reflect my social concerns. If I was safe, or what you see as 'co-opted' into the system, I would not be writing things like 'Time of Inconvenience,' which is very outspoken against the right-to-life campaign. It says, 'I would go to war to protect a woman's right to choose.' In other words, I'm saying if you take the law away from me, that gives me the right, in America, to make my own choices, that would be the only thing I would pick up a gun to defend."

Would Nanci kill in those circumstances?

"I would go to war to defend that law, and if a woman's right to choose, and to do with her own body what she sees fit, were taken away from me, I would go to war," she responds. "I definitely would fight for my constitutional right to keep the boys in Washington out of my bedroom. As I say in that song, 'The right-to-life man has become my enemy.' When I do Voters for Choice shows for Gloria Steinem, there are always people outside with their placards and signs and shaking those rubber fetuses in the air and all that horrible stuff. So I would hope that by writing about these concerns and similar subjects, I am carrying on that great tradition in folk music."

Nevertheless, this "great tradition" is now only a thin thread in American popular music. And if it has been replaced, to a great degree, by rap and hip-hop, this development surely owes as much to natural evolution as it does to the fact that we now live in the age of postmodernism, an era that is more accurately reflected in these newer forms of folk music. Couldn't it be suggested that Nanci Griffith can never go back to Bountiful again, that this music she has recorded on *Other Voices, Other Rooms* will never again speak for a mass of people, as it once did, and, furthermore, that this entire project, at best, can never be more than a noble gesture in the direction of the past?

"If what you say is true, there are more reasons than those you mention," Nanci says. "Yes, rap music has picked up the tradition that folk music had and is now more the voice of the people, but one of the major reasons for this is that it gets more commercial airplay, whereas folk music is pretty much ignored by the music industry, particularly radio. It's there, but it's not being heard. So if it is being silenced at that level, it can't possibly speak for people en masse. That, I think, is more the problem than the evolutionary tendencies you describe, in art or in culture, though these, obviously, are factors in an overall sense. The point, to me, is that back when folk music was broadcast over the airwaves and there were huge festivals and record companies were pushing these albums, then it did go out into the people and speak for them. It still does, in terms of folk festivals, at least. But it has been supplanted, to a great degree, by music such as rap and hip-hop and even rock, in much the same way that the blues has been. Only a fool would deny that."

Does Nanci believe that the same is true of that market-driven beast called "New Country"? Wouldn't only fools deny that it is a long way down from Jimmie Rodgers and the Carter Family to neo-pop acts like Faith Hill? Even allowing for exceptions such as Martina McBride's "Independence Day," which focuses on the subject of wife battering, does Nanci agree with those who suggest that New Country has betrayed its social responsibilities and no longer speaks from the heart or, indeed, the heartland of America?

"Put that way, it has," she responds. "But the bulk of what I hear these days, in this area, is not New Country. New Country is Iris DeMent, Jack Ingram, Gillian Welch. And anyone who has heard Gillian's album *Revival* and listened to the lyrics of 'Orphan Girl' knows that she is writing and playing country music . . . that definitely also is social commentary. The same is true of Iris DeMent's *The Way I Should,* the album that has the song 'The Wall in Washington.' She captures the grief of the Vietnam War in two and a half minutes, just from the use of three characters, as in the mother coming to the wall in Washington and trying to find her son's name. Then the son comes, to see the name of the father he never knew. And the father comes. It's a beautifully written and so very powerful piece. That, to me, is New Country, though, yes, definitely, a lot of the other so-called New Country acts don't face these social responsibilities at all. Most are just hat acts and Barbie dolls. But then, any genre has got to homogenize until it reaches a point where it rolls over and goes back to the beginning. And I think that will happen in country music. I don't think it can get any farther off the road than it has, and I think it will roll back. At least I hope it does. Because I really do think that country music has lost sight of its origins. I'm not a fan of urban contemporary country music. It just doesn't have anything in it for me to listen to. There are really no story songs, and I never was a fan of that kind of rock music anyway."

With comments such as this, one can clearly see why Nanci Griffith has never been co-opted into the Nashville system, despite the fact that she recorded most of her albums in that city, now lives on its outskirts, and is too often mislabeled as a country artist in record stores. As with her experience with record companies' reluctance to release "Ford Econoline" as a single because they claimed it was "too radical," in the sense that "women can't sing about a woman leaving her husband and hitting the road," the fact is that Nanci Griffith undoubtedly arrived in Nashville at least a decade too early—if indeed she could ever soak herself *that* deep in the potentially corrosive Nashville game. With projects like *Other Voices, Other Rooms,* Griffith also is moving against the ageist tendencies that now dominate country music. And which could be said to be accelerating its demise, relegating artists like Johnny Cash, Willie Nelson, Tammy Wynette, and Dolly Parton to the scrap heap because they are over forty and thus, it's claimed, might "alienate the kids." This relatively recent development in country music clearly aggravates Nanci.

"Of course it does," she says. "It angers me that Willie Nelson can't get played on country radio. And it makes me angry that Loretta Lynn does not get played on country radio. The very music that made those country stations exist is not being heard. And Emmylou Harris does not get played on country radio anymore. In fact, you can bring it up to the present. Gillian Welch does not get played, nor does Iris DeMent. Country music television is better, in that it does not so slavishly follow the radio chart. But country radio really has deteriorated a long way since I first listened to it."

Nanci also sees the irony and injustice in the fact that the "grand masters" of the art of country music such as Cash and Loretta Lynn are now virtually ignored by country music radio whereas, in many other areas of the performing arts such as jazz and blues, it is the aged voices we listen to and learn from. "And I would say there is great pain involved in all this, in the hearts of older country singers and musicians," she says. "The Crickets are a perfect example of having been similarly denied in rock and roll. The Crickets, along with Buddy Holly, should be remembered together as grand masters, like a lot of those country stars you name. But part of the impetus behind these two albums is to do exactly that, draw attention to the masters of folk music. The same will be true of this book, I hope. You've got to 'highlight the sources,' as my dad always said. And that, as I say, is what both these *Other Voices, Other Rooms* albums really are all about."

another voice

JIM ROONEY, PRODUCER

Jim Rooney has played a pivotal role in relation to Nanci Griffith's career and music. He not only produced her early breakthrough albums, *Once in a Very Blue Moon* and *The Last of the True Believers,* but co-produced *Other Voices, Other Rooms* and helped choose the songs for both collections.

Rooney's overall role in terms of the folk revival of the 1960s was no less central. Specifically, he managed the legendary Club 47 in Cambridge, Massachusetts, which booked acts such as Joan Baez, Tom Rush, Geoff and Maria Muldaur, and many others. He also was a director and talent coordinator of the almost mythical Newport Folk Festival, which introduced to the world newer talents such as Joni Mitchell, James Taylor, Arlo Guthrie, Richie Havens, and Kris Kristofferson. During the following decade Rooney lived in Woodstock, New York, and managed Albert Grossman's Bearsville Sound Studios, where the Band, Van Morrison, Taj Mahal, Bonnie Raitt, and others recorded. Jim Rooney is a musician himself. He formed a partnership with banjoist Bill Keith in 1960. They toured as part of the Woodstock Mountains Revue in the 1970s and are now part of the New Blue Velvet Band. The artists whose work Jim has produced over the past twenty years include John Prine, Hal Ketchum, Iris DeMent, Townes Van Zandt, Jerry Jeff Walker, and Don Edwards.

Looking back on his origins, Jim claims that his "core belief in folk songs and folk culture" stems from that side of the divide which he describes as being more concerned with "the liberation of the individual" than with the "Woody Guthrie–like labor politics" that influenced earlier generations. This, he believes, is true of many folk fans who came of age in the 1950s.

"I am older than Nanci by fifteen years," Rooney says, "so I'm in the middle of these generational tendencies. But coming into the early 1950s, with Eisenhower and all that, was a very bland time, nationally," he explains, sitting at a metal table beside Nanci's swimming pool on an oppressively warm summer night.

"I came out of a background that was Democratic politics. My mother voted for a Socialist, Henry Wallace, for president, so there was that bias in my family. In fact, the first money I ever made on a political bet was betting on Harry Truman to win! I made half a buck on that. I didn't like the other guy. I never did like Republicans, have always been democratic in my leanings. But there really was this blandness in the general atmosphere, which was reflected in the popular music of the time."

As in what? The tail end of the big band era and the beginning of the "belter" period dominated by the likes of Frankie Laine and Johnnie Ray, which would soon lead to rock and roll?

"All that, but in 1951, although the energy of the big bands had just about spent itself, we weren't quite yet ready for rock and roll. But the very next year, through the radio, I got introduced simultaneously to hillbilly, jazz, and R&B music. And, to me, all this music was extremely exciting, spoke to me in a way that no other music had. Later I started to hear Little Richard, Fats Domino, Clyde McPhatter, that kind of stuff, and gospel music—all great. Because it was all very real, much more so than Jo Stafford singing 'You Belong to Me,' or whatever. The most popular disc jockey when I was in high school was Bob Clayton, and his was the most popular show listened to by teenagers. His theme song was 'Let's Dance' by Benny Goodman. And every year he would poll the senior class as to their favorite song, and every year it was 'Stardust'—that is until 1953, when the whole thing went down the tubes after Bill Haley and all those other people came along. And this seemed to happen overnight. Everything just changed."

Jim Rooney traces the folk revival of the late 1950s and early 1960s back to the beginning of rock and roll. But was he aware that RCA originally marketed Elvis Presley as a "new American folk artist," a title with which many people now agree, claiming that Presley clearly captured the cultural tendencies of his time, particularly among working-class people, as Phil Ochs often noted.

"I don't remember reading that at the time, but I agree with the assessment," he responds. "I first heard Elvis on a hillbilly show, *The Louisiana Hayride,* out of Shreveport. Every Saturday night the CBS radio network had an hour of live hillbilly music and he came on that, singing 'Blue Moon of Kentucky,' and I will never forget that moment. I can see myself; I know where I was sitting, listening to the radio in our place at the beach, summertime. Then I hear the velvety voice of the announcer, Horace Logan, saying, 'We have a young man here, and he's all dressed up in a pink suit, and his name is Elvis Presley, and what's it gonna be, Elvis?' and Elvis said, 'Blue Moon of Kentucky,' and he started singing. I'm not sure I'd even heard Bill Monroe's version at that point."

Monroe's original version didn't rock, didn't have the black and white cross-cultural elements suggested by Presley's title at the time, "the Hillbilly Cat." The slang term "hillbilly" designated the white country music culture while "cat" designated African American culture.

"Of course it didn't! It was pure bluegrass, but then Bill went back and recorded it again after he heard Elvis's version and just said, 'I liked it, man. It led to me getting some powerful royalty checks!'" Jim responds, laughing.

"So there you had evidence of how Elvis changed folk culture almost immediately, by mixing up black and white musical influences. But in the beginning, Elvis was presented in a country music context with a folk base. Yet he was totally different. And 'Blue Moon of Kentucky' was his country tune on the flip side of Arthur Crudup's blues 'That's All Right, Mama,' which was the same mix of black and white right there, on one record. And I'm sure there was a lot of resistance to him mixing things up like that, but you couldn't deny the public. They went crazy for him and for this music from the beginning. You could hear that on the radio, from the audience at *The Louisiana Hayride.* Artists who worked at the *Hayride* at the time said it was electrifying what he was doing. That's where it all began. And as I say, I'll never forget that moment. That was when I discovered rockabilly. I loved it from the beginning. And there is no doubt in my mind that this was an authentic American folk music, though I never really did get into worrying too much about labels. My real hero at the time was Hank Williams, who was important to any adolescent at that stage, especially if you were having your heart broken every other second. He spoke to me like crazy! I adored Hank Williams, and it was made all the more tragic that he died. I wrote to his sister. I wanted to write a book about Hank in my teens. I got all those 78's, and that was it for me. I was gone. Still am, when it comes to Hank."

A few years after Hank's death, salvation of a kind came when Jim Rooney discovered folk music, thanks to a friend of "Cowboy" Jack Clement, who produced and engineered many of the original rockabilly cuts at Sun Records.

"I got into folk music when a promoter, Aubrey Meyhew, got me on the radio, at the age of sixteen as a DJ," Jim recalls, referring to his 1954 debut on Boston's WCOP *Hayloft Jamboree.*

"Around the same time, I was wandering around Boston one day and found this little store called the Book Clearing House, and they had a couple of bins of records in the back—Folkways, Riverside LPs. I bought Leadbelly's last session, Big Bill Broonzy, a compilation of American banjo music that Mike Seeger put together. Stuff like that. I had bought myself a Martin guitar so I'd be at home with my Hank Williams records and these new records, and I learned some of those Leadbelly tunes. I learned 'Big Bill Broonzy.' And my mother gave me a book, *American Songbag* by Carl Sandburg. I'd go through that, find something that appealed to me, make up melodies to these songs. I was totally on my own. I had no outlet to perform, nothing like that. And through Symphony Syd on Boston radio and this club called Storyville, I'd become more aware of jazz and went to see people like Duke Ellington, which was really something else! Me and another kid from school were the only white people in there, apart from the maître d' and the bartender! It was a benefit for the NAACP. I didn't even know what that was, at sixteen! But all these great jazz musicians were there—Harry Carney from Dorchester, Paul Gonzales from Pittucket, Johnny Hodges from Cambridge—and it was the hippest place to be in the city of Boston on that day. So, having become aware of jazz, I then, naturally enough, gravitated toward a couple of beatniks I met in college. And they had Miles Davis and Thelonious Monk, so I started buying those records." Like folk snobs, many of the beatniks who tuned in to Miles and Monk despised rock and roll. By the late 1950s Jim Rooney began to develop similar tendencies.

"As far as I was concerned, people like Elvis, Fats Domino, and Jerry Lee Lewis were happening but then immediately it got co-opted, with Fabian, Pat Boone, all that." Jim grimaces. "That music and Paul Anka had absolutely nothing to say to me. The Everly Brothers did. I copped to them immediately, but I was in college in western Massachusetts by that stage, and I might as well have gone to the moon. There was no TV, no radio; we lived a very insulated life out there. But what we did have was our records. These hipsters had jazz, and I had hillbilly and folk music. And that, to me, was the beginning of what I now see was a form of counterculture."

And Rooney was in there from the outset, he claims.

"In college I met this kid, Bill Keith, and he was learning how to play banjo, and I was singing Hank Williams's songs and had an electric band behind me! I didn't take no vows of purity! So a friend of ours put Bill and me together, and that's the kind of stuff we did." He smiles fondly at the memory.

"And when two friends of ours got thrown out of college for being underachievers, they went down to Cambridge and we went to visit them, which really kicked off another major stage of the story. One of their friends was giving guitar lessons to this great-looking girl, and it was Joan Baez. And we then found out about all these coffeehouses in Boston, and on our vacations we'd go to these places, see Reverend Gary Davis, the Chad Mitchell Trio, all those folk greats."

On reflection, however, of far more importance to Jim Rooney were the cultural undercurrents which informed that music and, indeed, deeply influenced the development of "the whole counterculture," as he saw it.

"My class in school was one of the first classes of this so-called under-achiever tide," he says. "I had a teacher who was documenting it, trying to figure what was happening. But there was something that wasn't connecting with us. We were not accepting the program. We were disengaged—as smart as anyone but not accepting the whole social agenda that was being presented to us. Four years later, of course, this became a major rejection of what was being presented. That was probably what others would call the real, identifiable beginning of the counterculture. But in my senior year, we really were driven by this desire to fuck the system over and upset all the rules—such as all the golden rules about the fraternity, which we did, big-time, leading to the building of dormitories for the first time. Then three years after me, the kids who graduated in 1963 really started getting radical. And the kids who graduated in 1964, by the time the Vietnam War had started, were really ready to tackle the system, attempt to change things in a major way."

How would Jim Rooney define the abiding disillusionment he and his college buddies were feeling in the late 1950s?

"We'd achieved the middle-class dream and found it was hollow, it was boring, it was shit," he claims. "And the folk thing did have that political component, so even though we weren't involved with the labor thing, we *were* involved, say, in antinuclear events and then the civil rights movement. By 1963 the folk thing was a major force in the civil rights movement in terms of people like Peter, Paul and Mary; Joan Baez; and Bob Dylan."

Wasn't this whole movement predominantly middle class at the outset?

"Definitely," Jim responds. "We were all the sons and daughters of relatively affluent parents. In my case, I was third-generation Irish. My friends were third-generation Jewish, whatever. But we were all going to college, and a lot of us took this big left turn away from the prescribed path of being a doctor, lawyer, whatever. My parents had raised us to think for ourselves, so they weren't totally thrilled when I started running a folk club—my father thought it was a little frivolous—but then they went for it."

How committed to social change were Jim and his buddies? Revisionists suggest that the "left turn" taken by young people of his class and generation was just a fashionable rebel-without-a-cause pose, a phase kids traveled through before hastily moving back to embrace the status quo and thus serve hegemonic structures by becoming doctors or lawyers. Some even claim that many of these so-called rebels *couldn't* have walked with Guthrie, for example, in terms of labor concerns because they didn't really give a damn about the workers or civil rights for African Americans, and so on.

"That's probably how it was," says Jim, having paused to consider the question. "And I had that feeling myself. My own personal take on it was that there was something about telling other people how to live their lives that I never bought into. It was the same in terms of the self-righteous aspect of it all. Boston has always been a hotbed of self-righteousness, and people in the North are always ready to tell people in the South, in particular, what to do. Boston is one of the most racist cities I've ever lived in, and, sad to say, some of the most virulent racists are Irish-American. But because Bill [Keith] and I were interested in this music, we went to North Carolina and began playing with people who didn't share our views about race and other things. Being racist was their culture, but I wasn't about to preach to them about anything. However, if somebody said something overtly racist, I'd let them know it was not something I agreed with. Yet some people did say, 'How could you even contemplate associating with people like that?' Well, 'people like that' are people, and I am a firm believer in human contact being the way we solve these problems. We will not solve problems by ostracizing our opposites. However, that said, there were virulent racists at that point in time, and the only thing they understood was real confrontation."

Where does Jim stand in the argument that Bob Dylan was the quintessential middle-class kid who played with politics and, by extension, toyed with the concerns of the people, simply to launch his career, before retreating into a more solipsistic mode? And how does he feel about the claim that young people in the 1960s allowed themselves to be neutralized on a political level by thinking that by simply singing, for example, "The Times They Are a-Changin'" was as effective a gesture as getting out there and working to actually change the structures and institutions that shape society? Isn't this the criticism cynics have always leveled against "political" folk music in general, going back through the Freedom Singers' Society in the 1930s and to the publication of *Socialist Songs with Music* by the Wobblies (the International Workers of the World) in 1901?

"Whether people were 'playing' with politics or not, they still had a pretty big impact on the culture, and they did contribute to change. And music was, as I say, an element of it, particularly someone like Dylan," Jim responds. "But to me the big thing, culturally and, in a sense, politically, was meeting the musicians from an earlier generation whom we brought into our clubs and, in some cases, into our homes. Like Mississippi John Hurt, Sonhouse, Doc Watson, Maybelle Carter, all those. And all that came about through the Harry Smith anthology, the Lomax work, and the fact that the Newport Folk Festival had on its board people like Alan Lomax and Mike Seeger, who were collectors. The first Newport Folk Festival was in 1959, I think. And then Pete Seeger did it in a nonprofit way in 1962, with a board of directors, focusing on the traditions, the music, on bringing 'real' folk artists to the festival as well as the stars. And everybody got the same pay! Fifty bucks per day, plus your expenses. Equality! We'd put you up in the college dormitory, and if you wanted to stay in the Viking Hotel, you'd pay for it yourself. And everybody accepted that because it was Pete Seeger doing the asking. So Peter, Paul and Mary, fifty bucks, stayed in the Viking Hotel. Bob Dylan, fifty dollars, stayed in the Viking."

Jim Rooney suddenly laughs. "But you know what?" he says. "While they were over there, we were in the dormitories with Bill Monroe and Muddy Waters and Doc Watson, and we had parties at night, having a ball! And it was an incredible experience, a total bonding thing between all these people of different generations, from different parts of the country, from other countries. We had Ewan McColl, Seamus Ennis, from England, Ireland. We went out and got the real people, and as I was connected to the younger people, it was also up to me to see we had the younger, newer acts. We had Joni Mitchell, Van Morrison, Gordon Lightfoot, all during the time I was there, throughout the 1960s. And the thing is that if we got people like Mississippi John Hurt up there at Newport, I could have them in Club 47 beforehand, afterward, give them a week's worth of work out of that. And while playing there, guys who never heard blues music were playing with blues artists like Doc Watson. And they'd stay in our houses, become our friends. It was an incredible opportunity to learn about other cultures from people who were masters of that music. For me, *that's* what it was all about."

So why did the audience go crazy the year Bob Dylan plugged in at Newport, in 1966? Why didn't they realize he was carrying on the Mississippi John Hurt tradition or, like the act that preceded him that day, the Paul Butterfield Blues Band—simply checking out folk's base in black culture? Why did Pete Seeger get so angry at what he seemed to believe was this violation of all that was pure about folk music?

"Some did get angry, some didn't; some loved it, some hated it. For Pete Seeger it was too loud," Jim suggests. "But I wrote a thing about this at the time, because I was being invited to join the board, and Ralph Lenser asked me to come to the festival and critique it, which I did. And part of it was printed in *Sing Out*. But I didn't write it to be public, and what I commented on was that one of the things, which I've never liked about rock and roll, was the attitude element. Like 'I'm up here, you're down there, fuck you.' We never had that fuck-you attitude in the folk community. That is not part of the folk experience."

Is Jim Rooney suggesting therefore that it was Dylan's "fuck you" attitude, more than the fact that he went electric, which infuriated Newport audiences on that historic day?

"Well, let me put it this way. Bob had just come from England, and suddenly he's in shades, wearing a polka-dot shirt and high-heel boots and everything," he responds. "Though, that said, Bob always had an attitude. In 1963 he had a bullwhip he was crackin' all the time. And ridin' motorcycles. That was part of the deal, too, for those to whom James Dean had been a popular icon. It wasn't just Woody Guthrie who influenced Dylan! And of course he came from a rock and roll background too, played Little Richard songs in a rock and roll band, wanted to be Elvis, like most everybody else. But he fooled them into thinking, briefly, that he was going to be the next Woody. And in the process he blew Jack Eliot out of the water. Poor Jack. He'd been in England for a couple of years, and I saw his concert in Boston and he was brilliant, at the top of his form. Then suddenly there's this kid, and the next thing Jack is saying is, 'Wait a minute, this is supposed to be my big time,' and this kid copped his guitar style and some of his material—his whole Woody Guthrie credentials—and then is writing those songs! But Jack didn't write songs. He never got over all that, to this day. If you engage Jack Eliot in a conversation for more than an hour, somewhere along the way Dylan will come up."

So what was Jim Rooney's final analysis of what happened that day at Newport, apart from Bob Dylan's attitude? And allowing for the fact that, as Jim says, Dylan did have a deep passion for rock and roll and rhythm and blues as a kid, why shouldn't he have followed that path, whether it involved a bullwhip, shades, an electric guitar, amphetamines, whatever?

"No reason, and you're right, rock and roll was part of his roots music, but where the audience felt betrayed is that they somehow thought they owned this kid, had him all pegged," Rooney responds. "Previously Dylan had the little cap on and played the game, but suddenly he's got this new image, and it took the fans by surprise. But then again, apart from all that, it was very, very exciting. Because another thing happened, which was, as you said, Paul Butterfield's band played. And there was this big fight between Alan Lomax and Albert Grossman. We had these workshops in the afternoons where we'd do a ballad session, with maybe me, Pete [Seeger] as the host, and guests like Dylan singing a few songs, or the Everly Brothers and their father, Ike, whatever. But Alan Lomax had the Paul Butterfield Blues Band in a workshop, and he did a very condescending introduction, and Albert objected. Albert came up to him afterward and said, 'That was the worst piece of shit I've ever seen,' and before anyone knew it, they were wrestling around on the ground! Very entertaining times!"

Alan Lomax, of course, is the noted folklorist and onetime assistant director of the Archive of Folk Song at the Library of Congress. Albert Grossman was Dylan's manager at the time. But summarizing his memory of that fateful, or fatal, day at Newport, when folk rock was born, Jim Rooney describes as "extremely awkward" the events that took place surrounding Dylan's gig—particularly after Bob plugged in his electric guitar.

"Bob had planned and rehearsed this," Jim recalls. "So he did the three songs he rehearsed, and there was this brouhaha in the audience, and Dylan went off. Then Pete said, 'He's coming back with his acoustic guitar,' and there was this big cheer. That made it look like Dylan had caved in. But that wasn't the case; he'd planned that all along. He just couldn't find his acoustic guitar onstage, which I'm sure he'd intended having there all along. Then as far as my memory is concerned, he did an acoustic set.

"But after Dylan's electric set, *everybody* went electric! Suddenly everybody's writing these new kinds of songs and has got a combo, and the truth is, most of them weren't very good! That was the big change. Soon Jean Ritchie was even making an album with electric guitars and things! But to me it was all folk. It's the blues, real. And it was a defining moment. It expanded the landscape. That other thing was too narrow. But to this day folkies argue, like bluegrass people argue, saying, 'We better shut the door.' My argument is the opposite: 'Let's open the door, let 'em all in.' And I consider Hank Williams the folk artist of the century. So when Dylan went electric that night, right there was the big change."

And this change, folks, led directly to artists like Nanci Griffith becoming "folkabilly" artists and to Jim Rooney producing her return-to-roots *Other Voices* collections, at her request. By the early 1980s when Nanci first approached Jim, he had already written his evocative memoir of the Cambridge folk years, *Baby, Let Me Follow You Down,* had become part of his own rhythm section, and was working with his mentor, "Cowboy" Jack Clement, who wisely told him he needed "to learn about engineering," which led to his role as house engineer in Clement's studio in Nashville.

One of Rooney's first assignments as a producer was working with Richard Dobson, a singer-songwriter from Texas. That album featured Irish guitarist Philip Donnelly, who later would become an integral part of Nanci's band. Jim met Nanci herself at a party in Dobson's house around 1983.

"She'd done two albums and had some tapes and was already working toward a third, and we sat around and talked about that," Rooney remembers. "She'd heard the Dobson album, with songs like 'Ballad of Robin Winter-Smith,' which was Richard's song, heard Philip's work on it, liked that and the general feel of the album, which was very live, y'know? And she was at a point where she wanted to move up into something. She wanted drums, steel guitar—to move beyond the acoustic folk thing. She was fundamentally folk-based at that time—small, mostly in Texas. She had barely played in New York, and nobody really knew about her up there."

Jim Rooney believes that it is important to highlight the distinctions between Nanci Griffith's base in Texas and other folk centers in the United States.

"She came from a folk background. Carolyn Hester was the singer she admired as a child and that was the tradition she came from, but the Texas thing itself also was a huge factor," he suggests. "This whole folk movement was really a northeastern thing. Down in Texas it was a different world, and there was this group of songwriters who got started in a little coffeehouse and club in Houston that Townes Van Zandt used to frequent. And Lightnin' Hopkins was their guru, the guy from the older generation they latched onto. And Townes also had a great feel for the old English ballads. He understood the language and absorbed all that stuff. And there was the influence of Bob Dylan, in the sense that what Bob did was make it possible for people to think of writing songs out of the tradition, extending the forms. And Townes was the first one down there who did that, and he was just extraordinarily talented as a writer. Then people like Guy Clark and, later, Nanci carried on that tradition. Nanci had gotten her style from Carolyn Hester, but Carolyn wasn't a writer. And part of the Texas thing also seemed to be that they all paid attention to language. The language of their songs is really good. But in Texas they had this stronger sense of language and storytelling. Texas is a little like Ireland in that they do have this strong storytelling tradition, and those songwriters seem to have just soaked that up. It certainly is a factor in Nanci's writing. And they all read, studied the ballad tradition, as in the Lomax books of cowboy songs in North America. They paid attention to all that stuff, so when it came to hearing Nanci's work for the first time, I liked her voice, sure, but also the writing, which had all those Texas resonances."

Soon after this, Jim Rooney agreed to produce Nanci's third album, brought her to Nashville, and discovered that she knew exactly which musicians she wanted, how she wanted that album to sound, and even what style of songwriter she was drawn to.

"She wanted Lloyd Green to play steel guitar and she wanted Philip Donnelly," Jim explains. "And she wanted drums, so I got her Kenny Malone who, to me, is one of the best acoustic drummers there is. And I got her Pat Alger and Roy Huskey Jr., all those people. I also had become aware of Mark O'Connor, Bela Flek, as a result of my bluegrass connections, long before anyone else in this town, so I got those guys for Nanci, to give her music this brand-new flavor. And she wasn't just absorbed in her own writing. She listened to Tom Russell, Lyle Lovett, Mickie Merkins, and Townes, many of whom were part of that talented group of friends she had assembled in Texas."

Jim Rooney believes that when he made *Once in a Very Blue Moon*, it was not just a case of adding a "new flavor" to Nanci Griffith's music, it also was a drawing-together of all his previous experiences as a musician, engineer, producer, and folk historian.

"Well, it was the idea of mixing older musicians like Lloyd Green and newer guys like Mark O'Connor," he explains. "And another thing was that, having no budget to speak of, we were doing this in a 'quick-study, fly-by-the-seat-of-our-pants, let's-make-some-music-here' approach that also seemed to make everything work. And the atmosphere in Jack Clement's [studio] was a great one to work in because we had the songwriting tradition, the musical traditions, and the music history we were all aware of, in the broadest sense. So we weren't thinking of putting the songs in any small box. We approached each song as in 'what are we going to do with this? Who's gonna play on it? What's going to happen here?' And then we'd do it, without any kind of interference from, say, record-company bosses. Nanci was the boss. She was the person we were satisfying. And she had a vision for this album, though she didn't micromanage it. She also just let it happen, which is another great thing about working with Nanci."

What guidelines, then, did Jim Rooney lay down when it came to discussing the *Other Voices, Other Rooms* album?

"I resisted it at first," he says. "And I wrote her a letter saying, 'My instinct is to say yes, but my concern is that what we have done is so precious and good to me that I know we can't repeat that, and I want to be clear as to what we are going to do here.' And I told her, 'I don't want any preconceptions about studios or musicians or anything.' And she wrote a good reply, so I said yes, and we did a test drilling. 'Across the Great Divide' and 'Woman of the Phoenix,' the first two tracks from the album, came out of that session, no problems. And we were back in business immediately. Nanci paid for the whole thing, so we had no loss of control in any respect. Then we really got down to the business of picking the songs."

How would Jim Rooney describe his original vision of the album?

"Nanci definitely had the idea from the outset that these were songs she wanted to pass on, no doubt about that. She really felt people needed to be exposed to this music and they specifically needed to be exposed to the writers and pay attention to them and then go seek out their material. And I was absolutely in favor of that idea," he reflects. "When artists have a certain audience that's ready to listen to them and pay attention to what they do, the artist does have certain responsibilities. But the funny thing is, you do something like *Other Voices, Other Rooms* and it turns out to sell well, wins a Grammy, grabs an audience, and does everything you want a record to do. And more besides. *Other Voices, Other Rooms* certainly wasn't made with that so-called commercial intent. Yet, to me, it is commercial because it sold and connected with people and that's what I, as a producer, am after—to connect with an audience. But I never want to go chasing things. I want it to come out of the artist, where the artist really lives. And this is the place where Nanci really lives. And even these two albums are just the tip of the iceberg in terms of the number of songs she knows. Even that, to me, is pretty damn impressive. She also is totally committed to passing these songs on. And if that isn't folk culture, what is?"

Quite. And just as Jim Rooney's work on those early Nanci Griffith albums pulled together all he'd learned in the music industry up until that point so too the *Other Voices, Other Rooms* albums are a summation, but far more than just musically.

"Well, that's one thing about folk culture I've always loved, as in passing on from generation to generation the best music there is," he explains. "And I have been very fortunate in that, from way back during those Cambridge Folk Festival days, I had this contact with, as I said, older musicians from other cultures and countries, and I was able to introduce them to a new audience. I value that immensely, feel extremely privileged to have been in their presence and to have soaked up as much as possible of what they had to offer. Our turnaround is to pass this information on to a new audience, maybe Nanci's audience and beyond, so that we can even expand her audience somewhat. One of the best things about that Cambridge scene was that we did educate each other, on every level, as in me saying, 'You gotta hear Hank Williams,' and someone coming back at me and saying, 'Well, you gotta hear Thelonious Monk,' or whoever. And we did that for years! That, right there, was an education you can't buy at any price! So these *Other Voices* albums are an attempt, in particular, to clue people in and remind them, if they have forgotten, of Pete Seeger, the Weavers, Odetta, the Crickets, and also to make them aware of writers we feel are in this tradition, like Pat McLaughlin, Mickie Merkins, all these people. That, to me, is a service. And the fact that Nanci is doing her version of these songs in a way that respects the original material and also is an expression of her as an artist—while at the same time making full use of the various musicians who will make it as good musically as they can, and as true to the material as it can be—well, you can't do more than that!"

What, in essence, is the best thing people can take from these songs? A more acute sense of themselves, their politics, history, the knowledge that they too are part of the circular process involved when listeners participate in the creation of music rather than simply dissolve into the role of passive consumers?

"Well, there is such a range of emotions in these songs and so many states of being that it is hard to just limit it to any couple or three things," Jim suggests. "There are so many ways of looking at life here that it is pretty astounding. And let's not forget that, in essence, all of this is a way of getting at life. Me, when I learn, say, a John Prine song or a Hank Williams song, I am taking a part of that person into myself, which, to me, is an incredible experience. Same thing when you open to any of these songs by Nanci. And another incredible thing about that whole Cambridge scene was that it invited so many people to participate rather than just be observers. So, yeah, definitely, participation—that is what it's all about. In other words, if you're not the greatest guitar player or singer in the world but you can absorb this music into your life and sing it to your kids, your family, yourself, then you really do benefit as a human being. I really do deeply believe that. Really. And the fact that Nanci wants to pass on so many of these songs at that level is, to me, an absolute blessing. She has allowed these songs to come into her life, and the result of this is that she then is allowed to recycle some of this material in conscious, and sometimes unconscious, ways."

When Jim Rooney says that people benefit from participating in this passing-on of music, does he categorically mean he believes that music can, in the final analysis, make us whole, transcendent, make us fly with the angels, kiss God, however you may choose to describe that exalted state of being?

"Absolutely," he says, smiling at the glut of metaphors. "It empowered me on all those levels. It's given me a whole life. I started out by absorbing, say, the songs of Hank Williams into my life, right? But that was just a beginning for me. And that has led me into other cultures, made me more tolerant of other people, made me want to *understand* other people. That's why I say that the political side of the folk thing to me, on a purely personal level, is that the music led Jim Rooney, a person of Irish-American descent, to meet and mingle with hillbillies from West Virginia, black people from other parts of the country, Jews—all peoples. To me, that's what this music is all about. Crossing all those cultural barriers. And that journey continues.

"But as you said, the best thing is that true folk music really does release you from being a consumer to being a participant in all this, no matter how you choose to define that element of participation, whether you are a listener, singer, guitar player, songwriter, producer, someone who writes about the music, whatever. And I can't thank God enough that I've been lucky enough to have been part of music at all these key levels."

Focusing more specifically on *Other Voices, Other Rooms,* Jim Rooney finally explodes with delight at his involvement in this project.

"The best songs are the songs that change people's lives, and I know for a fact that the one album we've already brought out has affected people that way," he says, clearly on a roll. "Nanci has people writing her letters, and I have people talking to me, and they say that certain songs really changed their way of looking at things, helped them express feelings, thoughts, that had maybe been all tangled up. In other words, this music has entered people's lives in an intrinsic sense, and as someone working in the music industry at any level, you really can't ask for more than that—to be a part of making music that actually changes people's lives. And as naive as I am, I really do believe one thing, and this is that music makes you better. I don't know too many people who have lived a life in music who have too much to apologize for or regret, as far as doing harm to the world. As Pete Seeger said at the beginning of my book *Baby, Let Me Follow You Down,* 'Good music can only do good.' And Nanci Griffith's best music obviously is good, in that sense and in every sense."

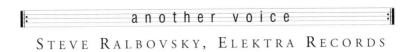

another voice

STEVE RALBOVSKY, ELEKTRA RECORDS

The first time Nanci told me about her idea for *Other Voices, Other Rooms* was at a restaurant in Nashville. I had just signed her to Elektra and was excited to help her reach the larger audience she deserved.

As a singer, her quirky inflections had such character and humanity. As a songwriter, her work is already tremendously accomplished. I did not expect the first record we did together to be the tribute to the songwriter that the *Other Voices* projects have become, but when Nanci started describing the first songs that she had cut with Jim Rooney, my mind literally raced with possibilities. This was clearly an opportunity to pay homage to all the songwriters that were meaningful influences, as well as provide a forum for listeners to learn about lesser-known artists.

The song choices were never obvious but always right on the money. The casting of artists was equally precise and fun. We talked that night for hours about our favorites. I realized that I had signed an artist with the idea of expanding her audience, and I couldn't contain the excitement I felt looking back to the musical places that informed my own sensibilities, and wanting to celebrate them along with Nanci.

At a time when many an artist may have smoothed out his or her earthiness to accommodate a broader public, Nanci turned herself inside out. In the process, she enjoyed the best-selling album of her career and won a Grammy for it. And she reminded me and all of us where the good stuff comes from.

2

the albums:
the beginning

Nanci Griffith and Jimmy Webb working on "If These Old Walls Could Speak" for the Red Hot Country Aids *benefit album project* 1 9 9 6

---

p h o t o b y
B e t h G w i n n

Nanci Griffith is correct when she says that the record industry regards "folk" as the *f*-word. So much so that one imagines most record executives would almost instinctively mumble the more traditional *f*-word at the merest mention of the genre. In such a hostile atmosphere, Nanci knows damn well how fortunate she is to have built up an economic power base that frees her to work on projects like *Other Voices, Other Rooms* without needing to resort to a record company for funding or support on any level apart from distribution. The fact that she originally funded the albums herself also meant that there was no record company interference in the hiring of producers or musicians and no opposition to her choice of songs, cover design, marketing, or promotion. For once, what you see is what you get of Nanci Griffith and Jim Rooney's original vision, compromised to the least possible degree. So how would Nanci describe the evolution of the original album?

"I was leaving MCA and moving to another label, though I hadn't chosen where I wanted to go," she reflects. "So I decided to do *Other Voices, Other Rooms,* and I paid for it myself. Jim Rooney and I did it. And it really did come into focus one New Year's Eve when Emmylou and I were listening to 'Across the Great Divide' and she stressed that if songs do not enjoy new voices to sing them and you don't pass them on, they die.

"I went to Jim because he had produced my earlier albums and has such a great love and passion for folk music. Also, throughout the years he has known most of the folk artists, and he knows what they did, which is something you wouldn't find with most producers today. And as a producer his essential talent is letting the tape roll and not allowing us to linger on something that isn't going to work. If, say, we record a song three times, he has a wonderful, magical way of saying, 'That's it, the second take you did.' He's very, very good at that, whereas it's not something I'm good at hearing. To me, they might sound the same. But then later I listen and go, 'He's right.' So he was a natural choice for this."

Jim Rooney also cast his clear, critical eye over what Nanci admits was a *very* long wish list of songs she wanted to cover in the *Other Voices, Other Rooms* project.

"The first list numbered about a hundred, because I wanted to do a song from every stage of the folk revival," says Nanci, smiling almost coquettishly. "But that was narrowed to fifty, then Rooney said, 'Now go sit down at home with your guitar and a Dat machine [a digital recording device] and do all of them and let me pick from that list to see what the best ones are.' We then chose songs that we felt I could interpret best and songs that worked well together, as in choosing, say, Buddy Mondlock's 'Coming Down in the Rain,' not just because he is one of that lost generation of folksingers but because that particular song works so well with Gordon Lightfoot's 'Ten Degrees and Getting Colder.' And that's how things progressed."

Were there tensions and gaps that Nanci has since come to notice?

"Yes, on both counts. I desperately wanted to do something of Paul Siebel's, for the first and for the second album," she says. "I went to Emmy in tears, with the first album, because I wanted to do 'Jasper and the Miners' and I couldn't get it. I'd put it down on Dat for Rooney two or three times, in a different guitar voicing, whatever. But then he said, 'Maybe you and Siebel's songs just don't fit together. Maybe you need to be Bonnie Raitt to sing Paul Siebel's songs. You're missing something there.' I went to Emmylou, who had known Paul for years, but even she said, 'Nanci, have you ever heard me sing a Paul Siebel song?' And I hadn't. So she said she'd tried and she couldn't get it. So I guess there are some things you are not meant to do.

"And there is another writer missing from these albums: Jimmy Webb. Jimmy and I are such good friends. I've recorded some of his songs for different projects, and he is such an extraordinary writer. We tried to get him to come in and work on the New York sessions, but he couldn't make it. Now, a lot of people may not see Webb as folk, but *he* does, and I do. People may think that lush orchestration removes his work from the field of folk, but I've never believed that point of view at all. When Webb does 'If These Old Walls Could Speak,' even though it's played on a piano, it's still a folk song. Jimmy also has that gospel influence in his music, which is wonderful. And Jimmy is a link in American music that is missing on these albums, definitely.

"Even so, when record companies saw the list of people who were involved, the cross-pollination of genres and generations, they were thrilled, with many, many labels wanting to go for this. They certainly saw the original album [*Other Voices, Other Rooms*] less as a folk record than an event. Everyone seemed to feel as Carolyn Hester did when she said, 'This is our own private folk festival!' And when it came to choosing a label, I chose Elektra because, as a child, I had more records on Elektra than on any other label!"

But what about that prejudice in the profit-led pop world against the *f*-word, which Nanci has often suggested is rooted purely in the belief that folk music doesn't make money, that it hasn't been profitable since the folk-rock boom of the early 1960s or maybe the singer-songwriter fad during the first half of the following decade?

"To me that argument never worked," she responds. "Time and time again it was proven that you could make money with a folk artist, from the Weavers in the late 1940s up to Dylan in the 1960s, Jackson Browne in the 1970s, all that. And, to me, that whole singer-songwriter movement from the early 1970s right up to today *is*, as you suggest, a folk movement, though you don't often see it referred to as such, because people still are afraid of the *f*-word! But none of that mattered to me in terms of any prejudice I might encounter with these albums. I was willing to put the first out, even if I never got my money back. It was important for me to prove yet again to the music industry that the *f*-word shouldn't be a barrier—that, for example, these musicians could be rock-associated but folk is their original base."

Nanci has already revealed that she took the title *Other Voices, Other Rooms* from Truman Capote's novel of the same name, but why, on the liner photograph for the first album, is she seen holding a hardcover copy of that book in what seems to be a pretty fair approximation of ecstasy?

"Because I am ecstatic!" she says. "That book was fresh air, a new style of writing, free-form, and so beautifully written that it was liberating on so many levels. It came out in 1948 at a point when things in literature had gotten really stale and the same pack of authors had been on the best-seller lists forever: Fitzgerald, Hemingway, James, Jones—the old school. But when Truman came along, it was a totally new thing, and he opened the door for a whole new cast of writers. And music was moving the same way at the same time, with the Weavers starting out. In the visual arts you had

Nanci on set of the "Speed of the Sound of Loneliness" video
1993

photo from Nanci Griffith's personal collection

the beginnings of Warhol; in theatre Tennessee Williams was knockin' 'em out with *A Streetcar Named Desire;* and in cinema you had film noir. In other words, the whole cultural landscape was changing. And then there were the beatniks, with John Clellon Holmes's book *Go,* which predated Kerouac and all that. It really started something. And Truman Capote was part of it all. I came to all that as a result of my beatnik parents. All those books were on our bookshelves. And I read *Other Voices, Other Rooms* when I was about twelve years old. It really struck me as a liberating force, a new voice, a beginning of something new in my life."

Nanci said at the time of the release of the first album that she chose Truman's title for her own albums because of his book's theme: returning home. Four years later she elaborates.

"It's true," she says. "Because *Other Voices, Other Rooms,* as a book, really represented a sense of place. When you read that book, you can see it, feel it, be there, walk through the world as viewed through Truman's character's eyes. And for me, making the *Other Voices* records, as with the title of the second volume, *A Trip Back to Bountiful,* very much creates a sense of place for me. And the book itself is about that return home. There is that inspiration to return to the original passion that inspired your creativity. And not only do I want these writers and their music to be heard but also, as we said, to discourage the loss. Because if we don't pass this music on, it does die."

*Roy Jr. is the legendary bassist for country sessions and the Grand Ole Opry. He bega*n recording with Nanci on the *Once in a Very Blue Moon* album and contin*ued his work with her on the six following albums, including* Other Voices, Other Rooms. *He proudly followed his father's legend (Roy Sr. can be heard on the Dirt Band's* Circle Be Unbroken *album), playing with Emmylou Harris in her Nash Ramblers band as well as for the Grand Ole Opry, Bill and Bonnie Hearne, and the list goes on and on. Roy Jr. passed away in April, 1997, after a battle with cancer.*

3

other voices,
other rooms:
contemplating
individual tracks

ACROSS THE GREAT DIVIDE

Words and Music by Kate Wolf

*Nanci Griffith
and Roy
Huskey Jr.
1993*

*photo from
Nanci
Griffith's
personal
collection*

That song, as I say, inspired the whole process of passing the music on. Kate Wolf's records were going out of print, and all of a sudden people hadn't heard of her. Emmylou and I discussing this on that New Year's Eve kicked the whole thing off. And it really did feel like Kate was there in the room when we were recording "Across the Great Divide." When I listen to that song, I realize that my phrasing is even like Kate's and Emmy's voice is like Kate's and Lee Satterfield's voice is like Kate's. Kate *was* there.

And when that happened during the recording session I

97

really did get the sense that this album was something I was supposed to do. That and the fact that we never had a bad experience recording these albums. It was so easy. It is like all those voices who have left us were back with us in the studio, ensuring that things would go smoothly. Because musically, vocally, it really is so easy, like everyone checks their ego at the door and gives over the best of what they are to the songs. There are no stars there, apart from the songs. And being at that point of intersection, as one of the singers of that song that day in the studio, suggested to me that Kate was at peace with dying, before she even knew she had such a short time left. In other words, she wrote this song before she knew she was dying, which I always saw as ironic. Another thing about Kate is that in America she's always viewed as this pure angel who wrote these interior songs about spiritual growth. Kate was one of the wildest people I ever knew! That's what you and I were talking about earlier—folk music denying the life, the body, sexuality. Kate certainly didn't do that. She was married several times!

WOMAN OF THE PHOENIX

Words and Music by Vince Bell
This song is also about rising up from the ashes. And Vince Bell is such a phenomenal songwriter, from that same generation as Steve Earle, Lucinda Williams—that whole generation of writers who followed Guy Clark and Townes Van Zandt around. But what I love about this song is the fact that even though Vince wrote this as a man, he knew that a woman of the phoenix was what he needed in his own life. He also is one of those male writers who are well able to capture, in their art, the soul of a woman. Then again, I do happen to believe that the soul is genderless. Or rather, all genders. That's something that goes back to when I began reading Larry McMurtry and realized how amazing it was that this man could evoke a woman's emotions and thoughts to such a profound degree. The same applies to Adam Duritz, on the first Counting Crows album, *August and Everything After*. The best songwriters work from that essence of being. As in Vince, with "Woman of the Phoenix."

What made that session so special was that Vince had a terrible car crash fourteen years ago, was in a coma for six months, and when he came out of it, it was a case of total amnesia, back to infancy. He had to relearn everything. It took him ten years to relearn all his songs and how to play piano, then develop the skill to write again. So Lyle Lovett and I and all the Texas artists would sing Vince's songs, and in that sense knew we had him in a safe place. So for us it was really important to carry Vince's songs around with us, as in me saying to Lyle, or whomever, "You maintain this chapter, I'll hold this one!" That was the sweet thing about recording this particular song. This was my chapter to carry forward! And Vince was really moved by that.

TECUMSEH VALLEY

Words and Music by Townes Van Zandt
The fact that Townes described this as the best recording of the song really means so much to me, especially since I relate so much to the protagonist of the song, Caroline. Townes's praise and the note I got from him after I recorded the song, when he said he treasured this recording, were so special to me. He sent me this fax saying "*God bless* Caroline." To think Townes would do that really made my day. He was such a sweet man.

And Arlo and I did, as I told you, cry our way through this recording, because it really reconnected me to my roots, and reconnected Arlo to Oklahoma. Totally. You can hear us crying on the recording. He wanders off pitch; so do I. We just couldn't help it. And the musicians who were there, like James Hooker, said he hardly made it through the recording, could barely see his keyboard. And all this was long before Townes died. This song has always been a favorite of my audience.

THREE FLIGHTS UP

Words and Music by Frank Christian
I chose this because I love the lilt to it. It's a very sad song—two people parting company but parting on good terms, cherishing the passion they shared, celebrating that. Frank Christian also happens to be one of the most incredible acoustic guitar players I've ever met. His talent . . . comes across on this track; he was happy as hell just to play and not have to sing. But he not only writes great songs; he also is a preserver of Delta blues and country blues—for example, the songs of Robert Johnson and Willie McTell. In his own playing he passes on how they played those songs. On all those levels he's always fascinated me.

Nanci and Emmylou Harris
NASHVILLE, 1997

photo by Alan Messer

Arlo Guthrie
1992

"Tecumseh Valley"
photo from
Nanci Griffith's
personal collection

Frank Christian,
songwriter of
"Three Flights Up,"
at the New York
session for Other
Voices, Other Rooms
1996

photo by
Alan Messer

100

Words and Music by Bob Dylan

There was a choice between doing two Dylan songs for this album, "Boots of Spanish Leather" or "You're Gonna Make Me Lonesome (When You Go)." Those two are both so special, so human, so profound. "Boots of Spanish Leather" is remarkable. It's just a correspondence between two people, and there is no repeat, no chorus, no hook, until the very last line. But "You're Gonna Make Me Lonesome" also has a beautiful melody and all those wonderful references to literature, as in Rimbaud. The beauty of describing this person in terms of "crickets chirping back and forth in rhyme" is just so evocative.

I've always loved "Boots of Spanish Leather." It has no chorus, is five minutes long, and is a classic example of how some of Bob's stuff is really hard to play! Even as a guitarist he's more innovative than he's usually given credit for, especially in terms of his voicings. Bob would find an unusual placement for his fingers and create augmentations of a chord that no one else had ever used. Or he'd use a chord you had not heard in that context. He pulled together country and folk and blues elements in his music in that sense too, though this, as I say, is far less well celebrated than the innovative approach he brought to lyrics. Musically, he crossed many barriers.

Dylan dubbed in his harmonica part on this track because he couldn't make it to the session. I was going to go out to Los Angeles, but Bob called and said, "Why don't you just send me the tape? Because it might be three o'clock in the morning when I get the time to do this. And that way I'm not disturbing your schedule." We trusted him, because it is, after all, his song. But it was something he definitely wanted to do, because he had not put a harmonica on it the first time around. So we got the tape back, put it on the reel, and it was just gorgeous. Especially the closing note: Mr. Dylan gets the last word!

As someone who grew up with Dylan's music being such a big part of my childhood, it's great to have him praise my work. He loved my *Once in a Very Blue Moon* album and the song "From a Distance." He once said, "When I got your *Lone Star State of Mind* album and heard your version of 'From a Distance,' I wanted to record it, but then a whole bunch of people started doing it, so I realized I couldn't!" At his thirtieth anniversary party I did "Boots of Spanish Leather" because he asked me to. I am incredibly respectful of who Dylan is and how he's helped the rest of us to do what we do. I think of him in epic terms, in relation to his role in folk music.

What I also love about Dylan is that, like Townes Van Zandt, he was never afraid to expose himself as a truly loving and vulnerable man, which meant he was free to write tender songs like this one, where he reveals he loves someone but has to let her go. Then he can turn around and write a vengeful love song like "Idiot Wind" or, earlier in his career, "It Ain't Me, Babe." Just think of that line in "Idiot Wind," which says, "I don't even want to touch the books you've read." That is truly extraordinary stuff. Though if I had wanted to record one of Dylan's more vengeful songs it would probably have been "Just like Tom Thumb's Blues," which is probably more of a bitter song than a hateful song.

He's great at writing bitter songs. And that, fundamentally, is what I realized when I first heard Dylan—that you can express anything in songs. He took Woody's writing to a more internal place, rather than it just being observational, social commentary. So what I learned most of all from Dylan is that you can write about feelings and still write fiction and still create characters, through observing other people's feelings.

SPEED OF THE SOUND OF LONELINESS

Words and Music by John Prine
John Prine is often compared to Dylan, but they are very, very different, musically. But I do think that John Prine's music will be around as long as Bob Dylan's. They're both going to be hailed as great writers of this century. But John makes it sound so easy and plays guitar and sings like everybody does! His melodies are so accessible and memorable. Once you hear a John Prine song you never forget it.

I chose this particular song because it says, in so few words, that someone clearly doesn't know what they are doing, spiritually, emotionally. In fact, what John Prine says has been said about me so many times! Like "Nanci's out on the road because she doesn't want to come home, doesn't want to face reality"! And that line, "Out there running just to be on the run," is such a great line that I borrowed it from John for my favorite song on *Blue Roses from the Moons,* which is "Not My Way Home." I wrote, "You'll be out there running. I'll be here to be still." It's the same idea.

Recording this with John was easy because we had worked together so much on these tours and so on. It's such fun to work with John. And for "Speed of the Sound of Loneliness" I threw in those little high angels singing "lonely," and he's asking, "Is that going to work?"

In the video for "Speed of the Sound of Loneliness" we did a takeoff of *Wings of Desire,* wearing wings made of real feathers. During the filming we were walking through a cemetery in Nashville and realized that people in cars driving by couldn't see the film crew. They just saw these life-size angels strolling around! At one point the wind caught my wings, and because I'm so light, I was literally about to take flight, and John was calling, "Come back down! Come back down!" And we could hear the squeal of car tires as drivers passed the cemetery. It was probably people saying, "Ma, did you see that? Nanci Griffith and John Prine! And they're angels! When did they die?"

But, more seriously, that was John's first music video, and it really helped kick his career onto another plateau. And what was really great about the success of *Other Voices, Other Rooms* was that people like Vince Bell, Townes Van Zandt, and Carolyn Hester had new interest shown in their work. Carolyn's old albums have been reissued, which is exactly what I was hoping would happen when we recorded these songs. People are going back and checking out the original artists, the original songs. That is such a real thrill to me.

FROM CLARE TO HERE

Words and Music by Ralph McTell
I had not heard, since Ralph McTell's recording, this song done in the context of the original—in terms of the slowness and the beauty of the guitar work, for example. Every time I heard it since then it was jumpy, like a bluegrass tune. And something of Ralph's definitely needed to be included on the first album because he was so important to the folk revival of the sixties. But "Streets of London" was done too often. And Philip Donnelly used to always do "From Clare to Here" on his own, after gigs, so I realized that's the way I wanted to do it. Philip made it an Irish song. And the Irish connection is hugely important to me.

In 1986 I recorded "From a Distance," and then Maura O'Connell recorded "Trouble in the Fields." And I went over to Ireland and did that TV show, *The Sessions,* and it was overwhelming to me that people knew my songs in that way—as in they knew all the words and sang along with every song. It was amazing! And . . . "From a Distance" was number one! That

*Nanci Griffith and John
Prine during the shooting of
the "Speed of the Sound of
Loneliness" video*
1993

*photo from
Nanci Griffith's
personal collection*

*Pete Cummins
during the session for
"From Clare to Here"*
DUBLIN, 1993

*photo from
Nanci Griffith's
personal collection*

*Carolyn Hester, Tom Paxton,
and Nanci Griffith*
FOLK CITY, 1982

*photo by
Wayne Miller*

was like a little blessing to me at the time. Plus I fell in love with Dublin from the very first moment I landed there. It looked and smelled exactly as it had been described in Joyce's books. The energy level of the music community in Ireland at that time was amazing and reminded me of my hometown of Austin, Texas. Back in my childhood I was also very aware of the Irish music played by, say, the Clancy Brothers.

For this track we brought in Pete Cummins from the Fleadh Cowboys. He said, "I don't know if I can do this. I'm not an Irish singer; I'm a rock and roller." I said, "Pete, you can do it!" And he did! He's a great singer.

I started writing songs about Ireland the minute I got there, as in "I Will Bring You Ireland." So all of that now has become part of my folk base.

CAN'T HELP BUT WONDER WHERE I'M BOUND

Words and Music by Tom Paxton

Carolyn Hester and I were on tour in 1981. I was her guest, and that was really my break, although I had one album out already and was working on the second. But then, going back to the very beginning, I had met her when I was about eight years old; she, too, was from Austin. She always had a brilliant voice in folk music, because it was this beautiful soprano voice, but it also had this soul to it. Plus she could take something like a Gershwin song and make it sound like it had been written for Carolyn Hester. She had this great way of interpreting another writer's work. She is a magnificent woman. Anyway, at age eight I saw her play. She gave autographs after the show, and I had to stand in line. I had cotton candy in my hands, and my father kept saying, "Don't touch Miss Hester or you'll get cotton candy all over her!" So I was in tears by the time I got to meet her. And she thought I was in tears because I was shy and afraid of meeting my hero. She wiped the tears out of my eyes with a bandanna, which I kept, and gave my dad a dirty look, as if to say, "What did you do to this child?"

I ran into her again when I was seventeen, at the Kerrville Folk Festival, and she remembered me. We became friends when she took me on tour in 1981, and she remains an integral part of what I do.

It was Carolyn who introduced me to Tom Paxton, who shared the stage with me during one of her concerts. That's when Paxton heard me sing

"Can't Help but Wonder Where I'm Bound." And I was just in awe of Tom Paxton because of all the songs he had written! Still am. The saga never ends. So it was such a delight to sing one of his songs—particularly this one—for this album.

And what was great was that when Carolyn and I were recording this, Jim Rooney kept saying, "I need some separation here," because he couldn't tell who was singing what! Our voices were blending together. But I had studied Carolyn since I was a child, and even though my voice went its own direction, there are big similarities there.

Emmylou is also a big fan of Carolyn's, so you get the three of us in a room and you are really lost! As we are on the "Yarrington Town" track on *Other Voices, Too,* which is sung by Emmy, Carolyn, and me. There's three generations right there. And here we had the same problem with Jim still saying, "Who is singing what?" But that, to me, is what the album is all about—that intermingling of voices, past and present, to a point where you don't know who's who—in other words, all you hear is the song.

DO RE MI

Words and Music by Woody Guthrie

Of all Woody Guthrie's songs, this one says it all for Guy Clark and me. We both know what it's like to be told, "If you're not ten times better than that guy over there, then you better go back to Texas." We'd never sat around and done this song in a living room or a coffeehouse. This was done in the studio in one take! I called Guy one morning, he came in, we picked a key, and we did it in the first take. No rehearsal. We read each other's minds! But then, I was probably born hearing "Do Re Mi." And the social truths in that song do still resonate today. It's like Woody said, "Don't ask me to write a song about how I'm praying to get a better life up yonder. I want this better life *now.*" I love that idea.

At the time, Rooney thought we should do "Deportee," but I said, "I can't do it without Lucinda [Williams]," because I'd been singing it with her since I was seventeen. In that song I sing a harmony line from the top of "Deportee" all the way through. I never sang the melody. So we held that song back for the second album.

One of the strange things about "Do Re Mi" is that one of the few moments of tension occurred when we were filming the video documentary.

Guy Clark and I had a fight over what key "Do Re Mi" was in! He stormed off the stage during a rehearsal. But in the end, he was right. And I hate that! I had to apologize to him!

THIS OLD TOWN

Words and Music by Janis Ian and Jon Vezner

This came about because I called Janis and said, "I'm doing this album and I'd really like to do something of yours, but I don't want to do 'At Seventeen' or 'Society's Child'"—even though "Society's Child" would have been a good choice. I told her I'd rather do something more obscure, and she said, "There is this song I wrote with Kathy Mattea's husband, Jon, and I'd really like for you to hear it." So she sent me "This Old Town," and I fell in love with it, thinking, "Doesn't that fit with 'Do Re Mi' because it's about the dust bowl?"

And I thought it was lovely that Janis Ian, a child of Manhattan, wrote a song about the dust bowl. Jon's not from Texas, either, but they both got the thing right. And "This Old Town" does bring "Do Re Mi" forward to the present. That's why it follows "Do Re Mi" on the album. Such songs belong together on an album, just as others should be kept apart.

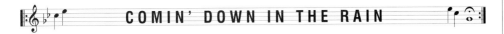

COMIN' DOWN IN THE RAIN

Words and Music by Buddy Mondlock

Guy Clark and I heard Buddy Mondlock at the Kerrville Folk Festival, and we both promptly fell in love with his music. Every time I heard him play, he did "Comin' Down in the Rain," and it's such a beautiful song. It belongs in this collection because this record represents what is good and should be passed on.

I wanted a new writer, a young writer, to show that a great deal of this tradition has already been passed on, despite the best attempts of those who would try to kill this music. And the fact that Buddy's music fits in with all this other music does highlight that continuity to a perfect degree. "Comin' Down in the Rain" doesn't stick out like a contemporary composition in the middle of all these classics. It's as though it could have been written in 1897 or in Woody's time or at the time of Dylan's earliest albums.

The same is true of "Night Rider's Lament." It could have been written three hundred years ago, and it is the only cowboy song Michael Burton ever wrote. Some songwriters have that ability to write songs that are truly timeless.

TEN DEGREES AND GETTING COLDER

Words and Music by Gordon Lightfoot

Gordon Lightfoot has always been a huge influence on my work. I have nearly all of his albums. But Gordon, like Ian Tyson, was more of a major influence in terms of style. He was so prolific, with an incredible volume of writing. But "Ten Degrees and Getting Colder" was always my favorite, because you can just picture this poor guy in the song, out there in the cold. And I always loved the fact that Gordon could tell you a whole story in two and a half minutes, that you could close your eyes and actually be there. In terms of the session itself, Iris DeMent came in after I had already sung the harmony part, when we recorded the song in Dublin. She originally came in to work on "Are You Tired of Me, Darling" with Emmy and me, and she stayed, so I asked her if she would replace my harmony on "Ten Degrees and Getting Colder" because I love the timbre of Iris's voice.

MORNING SONG FOR SALLY

Words and Music by Jerry Jeff Walker

This has always been one of my favorite Jerry Jeff Walker songs. It's from his 1965 album, *Driftin' Way of Life,* which also has "Mr. Bojangles," which, as you know, was his huge hit. I love "Mr. Bojangles" because it has a great narrative and is wonderfully visual, but I always preferred "Morning Song for Sally," and it's one of several songs of Jerry Jeff's that I would have preferred to become an international hit.

"Morning Song" is so beautiful. It's a really personal song about the sacrifices that a troubadour must make in life and love. So it's a good-bye of sorts. A reluctant good-bye, where you are giving up your personal life for music. But you accept this as the price. I have always related to its gentle message.

Jerry Jeff has said that he himself had forgotten about "Morning Song for Sally" until I called him to ask for it. We gave it a new life on this record. He now performs this song in concert again.

NIGHT RIDER'S LAMENT

Words and Music by Michael Burton

I first heard "Night Rider's Lament" from Jerry Jeff Walker. This song also has that wonderful authentic western yodel by the great Don Edwards, who always brought audiences to their feet when he sang that part during the tour. Michael Burton, who wrote "Night Rider's Lament," is originally from Alaska, and this is the only real cowboy song he's ever written. He was very good friends with Jerry Jeff, Guy Clark, and that whole group. But the song could have been written in the 1800s.

The part about losing your shares is a big thing if you are a native of Alaska, because if you leave the land, you lose it. That's why I always found that song so endearing and so opposite to what Michael Burton really is. He lives in London and L.A. and is very sophisticated, yet this song feels as though it could have been written by a guy of twenty in a cowboy hat and boots.

This song brings into the first album this whole area of cowboy music, as in western music, not country-and-western or country music. Western music has its own form of poetry, and this is what we really tried to highlight with this song. That's why Don is so right for "Night Rider's Lament," with that wonderful yodel.

ARE YOU TIRED OF ME, DARLING

Words and Music by G. P. Cook and Ralph Roland

I have always loved this song, from childhood. My dad's barbershop quartet sang it; I heard the Carter Family version. It's a gorgeous piece of work. And I was amazed, to go into the Library of Congress and find it was written by two men. As far as I was concerned, Sarah and Maybelle, of the Carter Family, had written it! I had no idea it was from 1877, that it had endured that long. And when I put that down on the Dat, with guitar and vocals, I wanted to take it to a different place than it had been before. The Carters' rendition incorporated a bittersweet "wildwood flower" traditional interpretation, but I wanted to give it a bit more definition musically, as indicated in the original sheet music.

Chet Atkins was playing with the Carter Family when they recorded this song. He was going to come in for my session, and it's very intimidating to be the only other acoustic guitar player besides Chet Atkins. So I put the

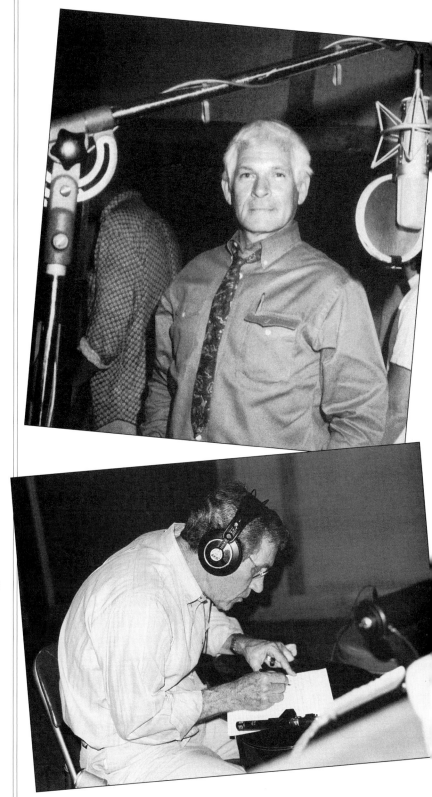

Don Edwards,
yodeler,
"Night Rider's Lament"
1993

Chet Atkins during a
recording session for Other
Voices, Other Rooms.
Chet played on "Turn
Around" and "Are You Tired
of Me, Darling"
1993

photos from
Nanci Griffith's
personal collection

guitar into an open G tuning and played a lead line, with just the melody. And I took that Dat down to Chet and also played it for him live and said, "How do you want to do this?" He said, "You're going to do that, as it is." I said, "I did it at home. I don't know if I can do it again." And he said, "You did it once, you can [do it again]!" So we sat across from each other, and Chet played rhythm and I played that lead, which is really complicated.

When it was finished, I put the guitar down and said, "Boy, Chet, you're playing the next one!" which was "Turn Around." But I did get, on guitar, "Are You Tired of Me, Darling," and I sang it at the same time! With Chet sitting there, with a big grin on his face! That was really gratifying.

The guitar part on songs like "Are You Tired of Me, Darling" are so darn complex they blow away any claims that folk music is relatively simple. For that particular song Chet Atkins *made* me learn my part. And if, after hearing it, there still is anyone out there who suffers from the belief that folk music is simple, listen to the melody of "Woman of the Phoenix" or "Turn Around."

TURN AROUND

Words and Music by Malvina Reynolds, Harry Belafonte, and Allen Greene
Malvina Reynolds was from San Francisco and didn't start writing songs until she was in her late fifties. But Malvina was an influential political song-writer. She wrote "Little Boxes," which was like the beatniks' theme song in the 1950s. And she wrote quite a few controversial "hipster" songs, so my folks loved her. She and Belafonte were always seen as very much part of the civil rights struggle; they were both political activists. But I love this song because both it and "Yarrington Town" are about a woman's coming-of-age. And "Turn Around" was used in a Kodak commercial when I was a kid, so recording it again brings it full circle.

WIMOWEH

Traditional South African Song   Adapted and Arranged by Paul Campbell
Throughout this album I tried to remain as true as possible to the song-writer's original intent. In doing "Wimoweh," it was vastly important to me that we didn't suddenly start singing, "In the jungle, the mighty jungle," and so on! I hated what was done to that song in the 1960s hit version, because people then didn't understand what it was all about.

"Wimoweh" session,
Other Voices,
Other Rooms
back row: Mary Ann
Kennedy, Emily Saliers
(background), Pam Rose,
Odetta, Amy Ray
front row: Leo Kotke,
Roy Huskey Jr.
NASHVILLE, 1993

John Hartford
tap-dancing during the
"Wimoweh" recording session
for Other Voices, Other
Rooms
1992

photos by
Beth Gwinn

112

Harlan Howard and John Hartford (engineer Mark Miller in background)
1992

Other Voices, Other Rooms

Ken Levitan, Odetta, Jim Rooney
NASHVILLE, 1993

Other Voices, Other Rooms

photos from Nanci Griffith's personal collection

Pete Seeger had found the song in South Africa in 1948; the Weavers recorded it originally. It was a song that the waiters sang in protest. It was not a love song, which is what the later version became. It was a protest song, like "We Shall Overcome." It meant that King Shaka, the last Zulu king, had died but he would come back and the people would rise again. That's what "Wimoweh" is about. So when they say, "The lion is sleeping," King Shaka is the lion. He was known as "the Lion." Therefore when the lyric is changed to "The lion sleeps tonight," it's not saying the same thing and that, to me, is a violation of the original song. The original "Wimoweh" lyric says that the lion is only sleeping and that he will rise again and that the people will rise up with him. So we stayed true to that.

The sequence of songs on an album is terribly important to me. It's like when you sew the whole thing up you better have a good knot at the end of that thread or it will unravel. So the last song is really important in terms of putting an exclamation mark at the end of the sentence. That's what "Wimoweh" is in relation to this album. This is the closing statement on the record, in every sense.

When we were recording this song, Odetta stopped the session at one point. She was like the teacher at the head of the class, saying, "Everyone needs to remember what this song is about." Then she said, "It's about people's freedom. Let's get to the bottom of this. I know it's not your language, but pretend it is. This is 'We Shall Overcome.' And that's where it should come from." But by then I'd already heard the history lesson, because Pete Seeger had called me and given me the scoop. As Odetta says on the video of *Other Voices, Other Rooms,* this song sums up the spirit of a time, a place, and a people. I hope that's true of every song on both of these albums.

My dad also felt strongly about this last song. It had always been a favorite of his. God, I don't know how many times a day he used to listen to "Wimoweh." And recording this song was really a thrill for him. He'd been in love with Odetta all his life, and there he was, standing next to her in the studio! Not only that but he got to sing the tenor part and do that little tongue-twirl thing that Pete Seeger did all those years ago! It was a great day for him—and for all of us. It was like going home in many ways, which pretty much states the theme of the book that gave the album its title. It was a perfect way to end the album. I always know, at least, how I'm going to start an album and end it. And we always knew we were going to start this album with "Across the Great Divide" and end it with "Wimoweh."

"Wimoweh" session, Other Voices, Other Rooms

b a c k   r o w :   Dave Mallett, Roy Huskey Jr., Jim Rooney, Marlin Griffith,
Odetta, John Prine   *m i d d l e   r o w :*   Amy Ray, Leo Kotke, Pat McInerney,
Emily Saliers, James Hooker, John Gorka   *f r o n t   r o w :*   Barry and Holly
Tashian, Nanci Griffith, Pam Rose, Mary Ann Kennedy

p h o t o   b y   B e t h   G w i n n

4

other voices, too:
a trip back
to bountiful

Jim was really eager to do a second volume, and when I put together my wish list of musicians nearly everybody I wanted was available, so we started recording this album in March 1996 and finished it in March 1997. It had impetus from the beginning, which was really inspiring when you consider how difficult it is to draw together so many different artists.

Each recording session—whether in Dublin, New York, Los Angeles, or Nashville—took on the character and personality of the place we were in.

The first sessions were held in Nashville, with the Crickets, the Blue Moon Orchestra, and Rodney Crowell. We did Sonny Curtis's "Walk Right Back" and then "I Still Miss Someone" by Roy Cash Jr. Then Pat McLaughlin came in, and we did "Try the Love," which was the kickoff for the whole project—three songs recorded in one day! That's what I

Self-Portrait DUBLIN, 1992

Taken during the Dublin recording sessions for Other Voices, Other Rooms

117

mean about it all being relatively effortless. Then we did "Streets of Baltimore" with Harlan Howard, the writer, doing the narrative. That was an absolute joy and made us realize that the album was going to roll.

The next sessions were in Dublin, where we recorded Stephen Foster's "Hard Times Come Again No More" and Richard Thompson's "Wall of Death," which opens the album, and "Who Knows Where the Time Goes," by Sandy Denny. Dublin was important because we wanted to bring in my favorite Irish musicians and also the British side of folk rock—for example, Clive Gregson, who used to play with Richard Thompson; Brian Willoughby from the Strawbs; and Iain Matthews, who was an original member of Fairport Convention. From Ireland we had Sharon Shannon and Mary Custy, whom I met through Sharon. We also had Nollaig Casey, who played with Frances Black when Frances recorded some of my songs for her solo album. Sharon, Mary, and Nollaig put out so much music during the sessions that, again, it was brilliantly inspiring.

On "Wall of Death" you can hear Sharon playing that carnival accordion and playing off Clive Gregson's guitar, and it is totally incredible. It also highlights my belief that this whole project is not so much a Nanci Griffith project as a group project, all of us musicians and songwriters—past, present, dead, and alive—all working together. That really is how I see the thing.

The Dublin sessions were so easy and magical. We had an incredible two days of recording, and then Dolores Keane arrived. I always refer to Dolores as one of my two sisters-in-arms in the record industry; the other is Emmylou Harris. I see Dolores as the queen of Irish music, just as Aretha is the queen of soul music. Irish music just seems to come up out of the soil, through Dolores's feet, up through her body, and out through her mouth. It's always exciting to hear her sing. And when I told her we were doing Sandy Denny's "Who Knows Where the Time Goes," she said, "Oh, God, I love that song," which fired us even higher. Though she also loved "Hard Times Come Again No More," she didn't know the history of the song and was so excited when I showed her a copy of the original sheet music, in Stephen Foster's handwriting.

The only other recording I know that doesn't shorten or homogenize the original lyric is Dylan's recording. Everybody else turns it into a "woe is me" song rather than a political statement. In fact, the song says, in so many words, what John Kennedy said: "Ask not what your country can do for

Richard Thompson

1 9 9 7

Recording session for "You Were on My Mind," Other Voices, Too

photo by Alan Messer

Sharon Shannon

DUBLIN, 1997

"Wall of Death"

photo by Gerry O'Leary

Clive Gregson

DUBLIN, 1997

"Wall of Death"

photo by Gerry O'Leary

you; ask what you can do for your country." All of this made the Irish sessions even more meaningful.

Then we moved on to New York, and that was a total change of atmosphere, though those sessions also were wonderful in their own way. You walked into the studio, and it felt like walking into New York in 1955! I had first met Dave Van Ronk and Odetta in 1981, when I was touring with Carolyn Hester, so it was extraordinary to see them again. Eric Weissberg, whose style of banjo playing has been so influential in folk music, was there, too. His playing is so clean, with no frailing.

Then, as we began to work together for this album we learned that there are a few complications in "If I Had a Hammer." It's not a plain white shirt! But Eric was great. He was only eight years old when that song was written, and he just happened to be in Pete Seeger's house taking a banjo lesson when Lee Hays dropped by, and he and Pete started writing "If I Had a Hammer." Eric just sort of sank into the woodwork and watched them! And now we had him right there in the studio, playing the banjo!

We also knew we were going to record that particular song for another project—a surprise birthday present for Pete Seeger. That compilation will be a collection of Pete Seeger and Weavers songs recorded by other artists, everybody from rock stars like Joni Mitchell and Bruce Springsteen to the purest of folk artists.

We also recorded Dave Van Ronk's "He Was a Friend of Mine" in New York. That was another record my dad wore out when I was a kid. And there sits Dave Van Ronk, ready to play on our version all these years later! Frank Christian was there, playing his magnificent guitar; Rosalie Sorrels was there, representing the generation after Odetta; and Jean Ritchie, who is seventy-eight and still has a beautiful voice, was also there and sang. The clarity of her voice is amazing. I'd love it if, when I'm older, like my dad and Jean Ritchie, someone brought me into a studio—just to hear that clarity—and if I could bring that clarity to them. . . . Those sessions in New York were really, really special.

Then we had the final session in Nashville, with Lucinda Williams, Steve Earle, Tom Rush, Susan Cowsill, and a cast of thousands. At one point, doing "Wasn't That a Mighty Storm," roughly forty people were gathered around microphones and we couldn't use headphones because there weren't that many of them in the studio. We finished up with "Deportee," "Wings of a Dove," "Dress of Laces," "Yarrington Town,"

"Darcy Farrow," "Canadian Whiskey," "Summer Wages," "You Were on My Mind," and "Wasn't That a Mighty Storm."

That was a full week of work, but it was wonderful throughout, mostly because of all the guests who were there. On the day we did "Wasn't That a Mighty Storm" we also did "Deportee" and "Summer Wages." Altogether there were eighty-three artists and musicians coming in and out of those sessions! And most of them wouldn't leave, even if they weren't working on a particular song. We really were having the most magnificent time. Recording *Other Voices, Too* was one of the greatest joys of my recording career. And that comes across on the album.

5

wall
of death

Words and Music by Richard Thompson

Joe: *Why such a relatively modern folk song to kick off the second volume?*

Nanci: To announce another journey and show that we want to begin with modernism, with folk music meeting rock music in the 1950s and 1960s. In that sense, Richard Thompson set the world on its ear. No genre can totally accommodate Richard. So we wanted to kick off the album with something that was folk-based but had carried folk and rock into a different room altogether. Fairport Convention managed to do that by taking what there already was of British traditional music and blending it with rock and roll influences. I remember playing a Fairport Convention album for my niece one time, and she said, "Wow, the synthesizers they use!" and I said, "Those are real strings, hon!" In ways like that, Fairport Convention was extremely innovative.

I always wanted to sing like Linda Thompson or Sandy Denny or Dolores Keane. Just to have that kind of power. "Wall of Death" was as close as I could get to that. I knew Richard's old band mates, Iain Matthews and Clive Gregson, were going to come in. So I knew Iain would be singing Richard's part with me, and Tom Russell would do the bass

Nanci Griffith
1993

photo by
David Gahr

123

*Brian Willoughby, Clive
Gregson, Iain Matthews*
DUBLIN, 1997

*photo by
Gerry O'Leary*

*Nanci Griffith, Brian
Willoughby, Clive
Gregson (in background)*
DUBLIN, 1997

*"Who Knows Where
the Time Goes"*
*photo by
Gerry O'Leary*

part. And somehow it seems okay that I sang a third higher than Linda and that I can't really sing like her or Dolores or Sandy. But it was so much fun recording this that we didn't want the song to end! Iain and I didn't rehearse anything. It was amazing how our phrasing matched. But then, I have listened to that *Shoot Out the Lights* album of Richard and Linda Thompson's so many times that I know every nuance, every phrasing of "Wall of Death." So did Iain. Richard Thompson didn't want to sing that song again; it was a place he didn't want to revisit. It was the same with the *Other Voices* project: apart from a few exceptions like Bob Dylan and John Prine, most people didn't want to work on their own material. In that sense, too, it was other voices bringing themselves to other rooms for this project.

Joe: *Is there anything about the imagery in the lyric of "Wall of Death" that reminds you of the work of Townes Van Zandt?*

Nanci: Yes. Definitely. I actually ran into Townes one night in Houston when they were closing the amusement park. A friend and I wanted to ride the roller coaster one last time before it closed. This was fifteen or sixteen years ago, and though the roller coaster wasn't a wall of death, it was the Cyclone. And the cars rolled up and they were all empty except for that last car, which is the most treacherous. But that was the one we were going to ride. So it rolls up, and there's Mickey White and Townes Van Zandt! Where else would they be? They came to ride it one last time and so did we, so we all rode it together, one more last time.

Joe: *So you see this as a metaphor for his life?*

Nanci: Very much so. He rode that roller coaster and the wall of death, in terms of how he took his chances and pushed himself in terms of inner exploration, so that the rest of us wouldn't have to go there. In that sense he was riding a wall of death.

After his death, I learned how deeply affected Townes was by depression. Although I suffer from depression myself, I'd never known about Townes, because he'd always hidden himself away whenever he became depressed. All the years I had known Townes, since I was fourteen, I never knew he suffered from depression. I wish I had been aware of that. I wish it was something I could have shared with him.

Joe: *But what can a friend or lover do when someone closes the door, in a physical, emotional, sexual, or spiritual sense? What can anyone do for Nanci Griffith when she descends into her private space?*

Nanci: Not much. You can treat depression with drugs and then walk around and be a wall of no emotion as opposed to riding a wall of death. Or you can experience it and take it for what it is. I usually try to turn a time of depression into a healthy thing, into a healing time. I write at a time like that, usually at the beginning or near the end. If I'm in the middle of it, I can't stand far back enough to write. That's just how things are at times like that, when the shadows fall. In that sense I guess I too am riding on my own wall of death. Maybe that is also why I tune in to this song so easily.

‖: s a m e   s o n g ,   s a m e   v o i c e :‖

Another perspective:
Nanci listening to playback

"In general, I don't listen to my own recordings because there is so much other good stuff out there to listen to. So listening here with you now is something exceptional. But when I listen to that song what I hear is Iain Matthews's voice and Tom Russell singing bass, and really putting the wall of death in there, really taking that gamble. Also, I hear Clive Gregson's guitar, which I really admire; it's so similar to Richard's guitar style.

‖: s a m e   s o n g ,   a n o t h e r   v o i c e :‖

JIM ROONEY

An interesting choice, leading off the album a little differently from what a lot of people might have thought Nanci Griffith would do. Nanci says this is to indicate a move to modernism, and I would agree with that. And the idea of a carnival being about thrills and spills. But, to me, the attitude to this album is just like that! Like just go for it and try to get it right. And I do recall Clive Gregson and Brian in the hall at the studio in Dublin rehearsing their thing, and they said, "What are we supposed to do?" and I said, "I don't know. I guess, do what you're doing. That should be fine."

Throughout the making of this album many people would say, "What has Nanci got in mind?" and I'd say, "I don't know, but I know it will work out fine." So there really was an element of improvisation and "Let's work without a net" about the whole album, and this song captures that.

We never listened to the original recordings at the session, except when it came to the arrangement problems we had with "You Were on My Mind." By and large we tried to approach a song fresh. But in terms of "Wall of Death" people, of course, had histories. Clive Gregson had a long association with Richard Thompson and he knew his style for sure, but we didn't try to do just covers.

PAT McINERNEY, PERCUSSIONIST

Working on this album is the most satisfying work I've done in a studio because the sound is stripped-down, word-sensitive folk music in the best possible sense. And the most gratifying sessions, for me, were the three songs we cut in Dublin. Partly because I'm an absolute Richard Thompson fanatic, and to play on his song was a thrill, especially with its fairground imagery and the idea of living right out there on the edge. I also love the way the song builds. And the other players on that session were fantastic. The guitar work with Clive Gregson and Doug Lancio is absolutely wonderful.

6

who knows where
the time goes

Words and Music by Sandy Denny

Joe: *Someone has suggested that it's almost impossible to listen to Sandy Denny's original recording of this song and not think of her death at the age of just twenty-seven, a life cut savagely short.*

Nanci: Yes, and so horribly, from a tumble down the stairs. It's like Kate writing "Across the Great Divide" and not knowing she was dying. In this title too, you get the irony of a life cut short. Another irony is that this was the first song Sandy Denny wrote. It really was a life cut short. I chose this song because it has always meant so much to me. I listen to it and I am in that season. I'm in winter; the song is like a cloak you can put on and hide within it. That's what the whole song is, to me. And of course Dolores Keane sings on that track, and the first time she comes in with that "Who knows where the time goes?" you know exactly who it is. It's like the ghost of Sandy Denny, an octave below. And Sandy definitely is one of those voices I would love to lead people back to, lest she be forgotten.

I've got the boxed set and, in fact, all the Fairport stuff. Sandy Denny really was such an innovator. It was such a loss. All the members of Fairport Convention were innovators and the tragic losses within that band, as in when their van crashed and Martin Lamble was killed, make it almost look like they paid the price of pushing the envelope, in every sense—pushing

Nanci Griffith
1992

photo by
David Gahr

the envelope in terms of what they could do, creatively; pushing themselves in terms of stamina, energy. They were literally on that wall of death. They were incredibly hardworking, gave themselves little time off, were hard-rocking, and unfortunately all of that took its toll.

Joe: *But what, specifically, is it about Sandy Denny's voice that, obviously, seeps into your soul?*

Nanci: Coming from Texas it was the first time I'd ever heard a voice like that. Of course I'd heard people like Odetta and Rosalie Sorrels, growing up at home, but it was the first time I'd heard someone from that tradition. It's like if you go back and listen to Dolores Keane with De Dannann there is something magical about the voice, like the soul, the spirit, of that voice driving through her body into yours. You can feel it. Likewise, you can feel Sandy Denny's breath on your neck, even though, like Kate Wolf, she now is dead. That's the magic of music. And when you hear Dolores sing, it's as if you can hear her breath. It's like listening to a solo album by Paul Bley on the piano—you can hear him breathing. So it really was the first time in my life I'd ever heard a voice like that. And it was so important to me, when I first heard it as a teenager. I just reveled in it. It was just an incredible place to hide.

Joe: *To go back to something we touched upon earlier, doesn't that inclination toward darkness also heavily influence which songs you choose for the* Other Voices *projects—songs like Sandy Denny's "Who Knows Where the Time Goes" are defined by their sense of longing. A lot of the songs you choose are prayers of longing for other places, people, times. Do you see that sense of longing as the soul of folk culture?*

Nanci: Yes. Longing is a thread that binds so many of these songs and that definitely is a huge factor in any kind of folk culture. And you're right, nothing expresses longing more than Sandy's song. Bring in the Dolores factor and Brian Willoughby's guitar work and you have longing brought to a fine art. And part of all that is that Brian was in a tuning I had never heard, and . . . the rhythm. All those guys playing together again, so long after a point at which Sandy had been the center of their universe, really does give the song an extra, almost supernatural layer of longing. You can really hear

Brian's anguish at the loss. He hits that guitar so hard that you know he's hurting and it cuts right through you. It just thrashes at you, like when Dolores is angry or hurt you can hear it in her vocal. Brian's guitar spoke like that, which really adds an incredible dimension to this song. And one that echoes with, above all else, their pain at the loss of Sandy Denny. And the pain of so many of us who loved and still love her.

Joe: *Aaron Neville once said he regards Dylan himself and Leonard Cohen as two of the most "beautiful" singers in the world because of this element of spiritual power in their voices, which he rates above everything else. Couldn't one also suggest that the ultimate beauty in art is putting a tongue to other people's silence, to paraphrase the poet Seamus Heaney, regardless of the technical quality of your voice?*

Nanci: But it's not up to me to say whether or not I do that for my fans. That's up to them to say. And I do love Seamus Heaney's line, though I hadn't heard it before. Yet that, to me, is what art should be all about— putting a tongue to other people's silence. What a wonderful image. Then again, that notion of a "beautiful" voice, in the classical sense, has never been an issue, in terms of the singers I choose to listen to. I could listen to someone like Tom Waits forever. He's never been much of a singer, in a classical sense, but who can deny the power of his phrasing? That, to me, is what is important. When something is phrased from the heart, you can feel it. And, yes, that is what I hope people would say of my work.

Joe: *Some critics, on the other hand, have said they hate the sound of Nanci Griffith's voice.*

Nanci: That happened to me a lot when I was with the Nashville division of MCA. In fact, the woman who was in charge of the radio division of the label reduced me to tears many times. She told me I didn't get played on the radio because my voice hurt people's ears.

Joe: *What is your response to your critics?*

Nanci: I just don't care what critics think. I do what I do out of love. That's about it. And if they don't like it, that's okay with me. Sometimes criticism

*Nanci Griffith, Doug
Lancio, Clive Gregson,
Nollaig Casey, Mary Custy,
Brian Willoughby, Iain
Matthews*
DUBLIN, 1997

*"Who Knows Where the
Time Goes"*

Brian Willoughby
DUBLIN, 1997

*"Who Knows Where the
Time Goes"*

*photos by
Gerry O'Leary*

does hurt. When they attack me personally, that hurts. You know when someone says I shouldn't have the right to record something—that's ridiculous.

same song, same voice

Another perspective: Nanci listening to playback

When I hear my own voice on this, I really like the softness. It's very relaxed. Though some people say they like the edge in it, to me my voice is much more soothing on these songs, a lot of emotion. Chris Ridgeway, who is our house engineer and who also works for Chrissie Hynde, is very good with women's voices. When you find an engineer who is as good as that, you want to hang on to him. I really don't think microphones, from day one, were made with a woman's voice in mind. Maybe they were invented by guys who thought, "Well, hey, women don't need mikes. What would they have to say?" But seriously, most women's voices have so much high end. My voice especially. Also Carolyn Hester, Emmylou. Same with Chrissie Hynde, who doesn't have much bottom in her voice. In recording such voices you really do have to be careful. Listen to the Carter Family and you'll see what I mean about old microphones. There are times when Sarah's voice would put your ears out! Same with a guy like Roy Orbison, who was meticulous about the type of microphone he used. He recorded quite a bit at Woodlands, where we record. One of the things people love about recording there is that they have all the old reverb plates.

But to get back to our recording of "Who Knows Where the Time Goes" in Dublin. That vocal hook I used was there simply because no one wanted the song to end. In fact, no one knew when the recording was beginning or where it would end! I just went into that, and everyone kept playing, so we just had to fade. In fact, I do believe that Brian Willoughby is still over there in that studio, playing on his own! When you get back to Ireland, give him a call and tell him the session has ended! But tell him gently!

JIM ROONEY

Sandy Denny was one of the best of that English folk-rock era. I've known of her work since the beginning, and this song certainly is her best known. The atmosphere of this song was really communicated by Nanci. And Nollaig Casey, Sharon Shannon, and Mary Custy, to me, really had a lot to do with the atmosphere, too. There's something very floating about it. It's suspended in the air, in a way, and that's how I felt that song should be set. I love the way everybody played it with spontaneous feeling. It was not labored over. We probably ran through it two or three times and then recorded it. So it was a very real feeling. The wrong instrument, or even the right instrument played the wrong way, can fracture the feeling on some-

Mary Custy, Sharon Shannon, Nollaig Casey
DUBLIN, 1997

Playback
photo by Gerry O'Leary

thing like this. And on this record, we had a lot of people in a smallish room, so if someone had made a wrong move it would have broken the mood, which was very fragile. But no one did. Everyone was very much in tune, in every sense.

‖: same song, another voice :‖
PAT MCINERNEY

I love Sandy Denny's work, Fairport Convention, the whole thing. That's why it was tremendously moving to cut "Who Knows Where the Time Goes" and hard not to think of Sandy. Everybody was thinking of Sandy and I can certainly tell you there wasn't a dry eye on the drum kit!

7

you were
on my mind

Words and Music by Ian Tyson and Sylvia Fricker

Joe: *In 1962, Ian and Sylvia had a hit in Canada. We Five and then the Cowsills hit with the same song later in the 1960s. In Europe the singer was Crispian St. Peters who, quite tellingly, cut the reference to drink!*

Nanci: All pop versions changed that lyrical reference to drink. When we were doing it, though, I sat down with Susan Cowsill, who was with the Cowsills in the 1960s, and she said they left it in. Still, it's going to be a shock to some people. And though I never heard Crispian St. Peters's version, I do know that many, many people had hits with Ian Tyson's songs. And as a child, I adored Ian, so it was a great honor to even see him walk in that door of the studio.

But Sylvia actually wrote this when they were together. She wrote it one night when he was out; I'm told she wrote it in the bathtub. It is such an unusual song, even structurally. They recorded it in 1961, and it was a hit in 1965 for We Five, which is probably where Crispian St. Peters got it. But I was just a kid at the time, and I remember that I'd close the door and blast the radio out loud because I loved that song so much. We Five did at least stay true to the original song, even where it changes keys in the middle of a line.

Vocally, it was very hard for us to record, but it meant a lot to Susan Cowsill, in particular, because although the Cowsills had the rock hit with this, they came from a folk background. Their mother had died a long time ago, but she was originally part of the New York folk scene. When Susan was at the session she said, "I really wish my mother was here now. It would mean so much to her to be back with all these people who were part of that folk scene." And we had these three voices: Susan Cowsill's, Maura Kennedy's, and mine. Then we brought in Tom Russell to sing low bass. And Emmylou Harris was there the day we were recording.

So we started singing, and my bandleader, James Hooker, said, "We've got a problem here." That's when he pointed to the fact that there was a modulation in the middle of a line in the third section of the song. Fortunately Susan is brilliant at harmony parts. So we played the Ian and Sylvia version and the We Five version and realized that the modulation was in the same place. We finally figured out that it never was a problem for Ian and Sylvia because they're just two voices. They never had to solve the problem of finding a place for the third voice to go! We Five handled it by having one voice drop out when the key changed. We didn't do that. We tortured ourselves, and at the end of the day, the three voices were there. But it was a hell of a challenge.

Joe: *Earlier, when we talked about this song, you mentioned the prejudice people exhibit against folk music, claiming it's all pretty basic stuff, structurally, though that is obviously not true of your own songs. But isn't there an element of truth to that criticism, particularly where the word is given a position of primacy, often at the expense of the music? Don't a lot of singer-songwriters miss out on the opportunity to add another layer of poetry to the song through the music?*

Nanci: Yes. And I certainly do think there is a tendency to be redundant, musically, and therefore to end up with a lack of balance between the words and the music, an absence of melody. But my favorite contemporary artists are people who realize and commit the melody and lyric at the same time and who treat both with equal respect. Like Indigo Girls who do extremely beautiful melodies alongside those magical lyrics.

Joe: *That said, Paul Simon has suggested that the age of melody is over.*

nanci griffith's other voices

Nanci: Not as far as I'm concerned. I'll always be a fool for melody, always be a fool for Frank Sinatra. I love a good melody.

‖: s a m e   s o n g ,   s a m e   v o i c e :‖

A n o t h e r   p e r s p e c t i v e :
N a n c i   l i s t e n i n g   t o   p l a y b a c k

Recording this song really was great fun, once we figured out how we were going to do it. And when I listen to it now I hear how we made it through that modulation. I also hear Richard Thompson's guitar, doing that lead lick, which is a little pitchy. It really gave it the atmosphere of 1965 because it's like "Mr. Tambourine Man." In fact, Richard's guitar lick is almost the same as the guitar lick We Five had when they had a hit with that song. And in my vocal there I hear me using a bit of Sylvia's phrasing, but that happens naturally, because you absorb so much of a singer's art, when they really influence you as she influenced me.

‖: s a m e   s o n g ,   a n o t h e r   v o i c e :‖

JIM ROONEY

This is a well-known song, and we've all heard it many times, but as Nanci says, when you get into the mechanics of the song, you discover that what sounded like nothing at all, sounded like a breeze, is really very, very difficult. And you come up with even more respect for the people who did the song! You can't help but wonder how the hell they did that—both the writer and the performer. In the case of "You Were on My Mind," of course, the writer was one of the original performers.

The harmonies in this song are extremely demanding, which we just discovered in the studio, and here again we were working without a net, and it was very challenging. People really had to pay attention and try to get it right. And one thing I do like about Nanci is her ear for harmonies. Her father was trained as a barbershop singer, and she has a wonderful ear for harmony, which is sometimes unorthodox. She doesn't necessarily do follow-the-book harmonies. And she got a lot of that from her dad. In this case we needed every bit of her experience along those lines, as in anything unorthodox that would work. And, in the end, it's really fantastic that they pulled it off. Now, I know most people listening to the song won't even notice that part. Then again, they probably shouldn't, because stuff like that really is the essence of art that conceals art, rather than drawing attention to itself just for the sake of drawing attention. There is a virtuosity to music that some people obviously appreciate, but the idea is to make it seem effortless. And I hope that's how this song sounds to listeners. But when we listen we'll remember.

Richard Thompson also played on this. And I love what he plays, which is another element of this record: putting people in songs other than their own. We didn't have Richard Thompson play on a Richard Thompson track. He played on this. But he welcomed that, and that was another interesting concept behind *Other Voices, Too.*

same song, another voice

S U S A N   C O W S I L L , SINGER

We did that song forever in the Cowsills. My mother, Barbara, sang lead. Mom sounded like the lady on the We Five record. She was only thirty-four years old. She really respected those folksingers like Peter, Paul and Mary and the Kingston Trio. My mother coulda been a contender, if she hadn't been so damned scared; she would have been right up there, I think.

Nanci reminds me of my mother, a little ball of energy. In my brain, my mom is still thirty-five, five feet two, hot shit, and sings like a bird. She had a great sense of humor and a cheeky disposition. Nanci winks at me like Mom did.

I told Nanci coming into this session that I wasn't sure what I was doing there, except that I figured out Nanci had been a Cowsills fan. She said, "It's just the way it's supposed to be. You're supposed to be here."

On a historical level I knew why I was there. But it was amazing to be with all these professional institutions walking around. As an adult singer and songwriter, having Nanci refer to me as a sister-in-arms helps me validate myself. For that little kid with that godforsaken tambourine to be invited to participate in this is some kind of confirmation. I marvel at the respect I get. It's humbling and makes me very appreciative of getting to grow and create doing it.

My mother would've loved to have hung out with John Stewart or Mary Travers, to have sung on their records. It would have blown her mind. And it's kind of cool, this many years later, me doing that. It's almost a vicarious kick for her. I'm sure my mother was floating all over that studio, singing along.

Ian and Sylvia in concert

NEWPORT FOLK FESTIVAL,
1965

photo by David Gahr

8

walk
right back

Words and Music by Sonny Curtis

Joe: *This, of course, is Sonny Curtis's song, with the missing verse that your heroes, the Everly Brothers, never bothered to record.*

Nanci: True! They wanted "Walk Right Back" so bad they didn't wait for Sonny to finish it! Then the Crickets recorded it later—the complete version—but this is its debut as a cover, which makes it, I guess, the "Whiter Shade of Pale" of its time. But in this case the extra verse doesn't change the sense of the song. In fact, it's as if I've been hearing that verse all my life because it's an extension of the first verse. And let's not forget that Sonny was very influential, as a songwriter, having started out as part of the Crickets, with Buddy Holly. But then, all of those boys wrote songs. It wasn't just Buddy and his backup band, the Crickets, though too many people do see things that way. And Sonny has deserved some credit for a long time. He wrote "I Fought the Law" as well, and dozens of other songs—everything up to the most popular TV theme song in America, from *The Mary Tyler Moore Show*: "Love Is All Around."

Joe: *Sonny Curtis and the rest of the Crickets, you've said, were rejected by the Rock and Roll Hall of Fame, which inducted*

The Crickets and Nanci clockwise from top: J. I. Allison, Sonny Curtis, Nanci Griffith, Joe B. Mauldin 1997

photo by Raeanne Rubenstein

143

Buddy but not his fellow musicians. That, you point out, is like inducting Mick Jagger but not the rest of the Stones.

Nanci: And that upset all the guys, understandably. They should be in the Rock and Roll Hall of Fame. And a few years back, at the Grammys, Buddy Holly was given a lifetime award, but they also left the Crickets out. You can't celebrate Buddy Holly's art without celebrating the Crickets. It was a whole sound, not just a voice. And even the songs Buddy recorded in New York, without the Crickets, they were still co-writes. They really do deserve credit. And J.I. [Allison] changed the course of rock and roll forever with that floor-tom on "Peggy Sue." But they don't get credit for any of this. I am ashamed of the American music community, in terms of the way they have treated the Crickets.

The session for this song was so gentle. Just listen to Sonny's harmony. In the Everly Brothers' recording you had just the two voices, and I did the two layers, because it seems that Phil Everly always sang that part of the melody we call the fifth, and so there would be that "you're missing the third" feeling. That's why you always strike that incredible crescendo with the Everly Brothers. Don would do the main melody, so there wasn't a third in there. Hence the Everly Brothers' unique ringing-a-bell sound.

On this version Sonny comes in with that third, and it's like a little pillow to put your head on. And Doug Lancio, from my Blue Moon Orchestra, played beautiful guitar parts on it. James Hooker also got on the Wurlitzer, to get that sound. It was magical.

This song takes me back to when I was five and first heard it. And I always remember that in 1954, the year I was born, Sonny Curtis and Buddy Holly were truckin' down to a music store and buying Stratocasters and putting their Gibson J-45's in the closet because they started to play electric that day.

Joe: *Now, Nanci, don't go telling me you heard them practice on that first day.*

Nanci: But I did! I heard them the day I was born! So between that and hearing Woody Guthrie while I was in the womb . . . well, is it any wonder people say my music is folkabilly?

s a m e   s o n g ,   s a m e   v o i c e

A n o t h e r   p e r s p e c t i v e :
N a n c i   l i s t e n i n g   t o   p l a y b a c k

There, right at the beginning of the song, is Sonny Curtis—"the pillow," as I described him! And James Hooker playing that little Wurlitzer piano, which is so sweet. I really am enjoying that! And it was so natural for me to record with the Crickets and to record something on maybe a first or second take.

That was the first session overall, and I felt like we tiptoed in there to see if another *Other Voices* album would work. We were asking ourselves, "Do we really want to do this again? Let's go in and try one and see." And this was a great cut to begin with, a great way to find that we did want to do it again.

s a m e   s o n g ,   a n o t h e r   v o i c e

J IM   R OONEY

Sonny Curtis is one of my favorite people, and he's also a very bright and smart songwriter. Though he is a little deceiving because his manner is so "simple country boy from Texas." But his songs are very sophisticated, which is something I really like. I got to meet Sonny and the Crickets through Don Everly. And I was very, very pleased that Nanci wanted to do this. Of course the Crickets are all from Lubbock, Texas, and I think Nanci felt a kinship with them because of her background. And there also was that sense of "look how far we've come" from, in some cases, a very humble background. Sonny once described his home as "a hole in the ground, covered with corrugated metal." This song is part of what got him where he is today. He was hot early in his career, when he was on his own, after Buddy Holly and the Crickets. And "Walk Right Back" is a great example of his sophistication in that it's almost hidden here. When you sit down to sing or play one of Sonny's songs, you discover structures in there that are musically really special and substantial but that don't draw attention to themselves.

SONNY CURTIS, COMPOSER, GUITARIST

When it comes to the question of what happened to that missing verse, the point is that the Everly Brothers just repeated the first verse because they were in a hurry to get the record out. Y'see, what happened was that I had been on the road with the Everlys, and I got drafted. And let me tell you I was doing some really serious hanging out with Don. He and I were pretty much in tune at that level—wild boys of our time, I guess you could call us! But we also were in tune musically, and I was in awe of him onstage because he sang so good.

Don Everly, to me, is just one of the best rock and roll singers, ever. He vocalizes so well; his pitch is so great. It's like a mixture of black and white, if you know what I mean. Let me illustrate this here. He curls notes like [sings] I-I-I-I [as in "I want you to tell me why you walked out on me"]. That kind of stuff. He bends notes all over the place, but not really just like rhythm and blues singers; it was more the mix that made it so new and innovative. And he was one of my very favorite singers, along with Ray Charles and Don Gibson, Carl Smith, Waylon Jennings. Country has played such a big part in my life, and someone like Waylon, well, his voice has got just so much . . . balls! Is that okay to say? You can clean it up if you want. But Don, to me, always had that special something in his voice, from day one. And with Phil, as a duo, they were unbeatable.

So anyway, Don and I would be talking songwriting, even while we were doing that serious partying, and I had the lick—dan-dan-dan-da-da-da-da-dan—ever since I'd gone into basic training in the army. And then one Sunday afternoon I went into the dayroom where I was stationed and wrote "Walk Right Back." They had a couple of beat-up old guitars up there, and the one I used was an old Stella that you could buy for nineteen bucks down at Sears Roebuck. It was a terrible guitar! But I took it and wrote "Walk Right Back." But only one verse. And it's really weird to look back on how things happened.

Let me set the scene for you. J.I. [Allison] and Joe B. [Mauldin] were living in L.A., and Don and Phil were there studying acting. I was doing my basic training and had never been too interested in guns, but I made sure I fired expert on the rifle range because I heard you got a three-day pass if you did. So I used that pass to go to Hollywood, and we all went to visit the Everly Brothers at Hollywood Hawaiian. And J.I. said to Don, "You ought to hear Sonny's new song." He called Phil right away and said, "Get down here. Sonny's got something we could use." And they worked on those harmonies there and then, and Don said, "If you write a second verse, we'll do it."

So I went back to Fort Ord in northern California. Later I had a nine-day leave, and I took that time to write the second verse and put it in the mail to them. But the next day I got a letter from Peggy Sue, J.I.'s wife, and she said, "The Everly Brothers just recorded your song yesterday." And I thought, "Man, they never got the second verse! They just went into the studio and said, 'What the hell.'" I heard it later on Armed Forces Radio, and it still sounded pretty damn good to me! I'd had songs recorded by Buddy and by Webb Pierce, but this was the best thing yet, and it really blew me away because they did it so well.

I did pretty good out of it. It was published by Cricket Music. Anne Murray had a big hit with it. Perry Como did it, Andy Williams, and now Nanci does it on her new album. Even without the missing verse it sounded pretty complete to me, but the song is copyrighted in the full version, and if, in a hundred years, someone wants to record it, I guess that's the version they'll do.

To tell you the truth, "Walk Right Back" always was, to me, a mixture of country and really elegant pop. Cole Porter and Don Gibson are two song-writers I was really into at the time. And I borrowed—I hope that's the best term—from both of them. I mean, Cole Porter blew me away—things like "You Do Something to Me." The chords in that song are simply magnificent. There are some movements in there, chordwise . . . man, this guy knew what the hell he was doing. And I was influenced by that. One song that definitely influenced "Walk Right Back" was Cole Porter's "I Love Paris." And, as I say, Don Gibson. I loved "A Legend in My Time." Great song, man.

But I love what Nanci does. She has that Edith Piaf quality in her voice in this version of "Walk Right Back," and it's something I never heard her do before. And the harmonies are unique, as Nanci says. That's why this is a bit more fulfilling, because we have Nanci and those other female voices, that fill in an extra added dimension to the recording.

J. I. ALLISON, DRUMMER

It's great that Nanci says the things I beat out on the tom-toms in "Till I Kissed You" or the paradiddles on "Peggy Sue" are roots music to her—and the roots of rock and roll. Chet Atkins has said that I brought tom-toms into a Nashville session for the first time. And he jokes about how everybody was usin' 'em after that. But I gotta tell you there was a Jaye P. Morgan record in 1955 called "That's All I Want from You," and on its back side there was a tune called "Dawn," and it had timpani playing [beats out rhythm and sings]: "Dawn is breakin' high in the blue." That had that "Peggy Sue" rhythm right there, way in the background. And I just thought to myself, "Wow, what good sound that is," so I took it from there. I didn't really invent it, like some people claim I did. Though they were playing single-stroke rolls, I played paradiddles on "Peggy Sue," and maybe people think I invented it because that was the first time they'd heard stuff like that.

It's like when Elvis played the Cotton Club in Lubbock, I wasn't too impressed by the look of the guy, but when he broke into "Good Rockin' Tonight" I couldn't believe it. I was in a trance. I'd never heard anything like that before, though now we know he took a lot of that from hillbilly, blues, pop, all that stuff. But, man, I ran out the next day and bought all two Sun records he had out, and I wanted to be Elvis! I was fourteen, and what impressed me was that he was carrying in the amps, helping people set up the stuff. And I was thinking, "Boy, would I like to play with him!" And sitting around later, I said, "Hey, Elvis, how come you don't have a drummer?" and he said, "Man, if I had a drummer it'd sound just like Bill Haley!" And there I was trying to get the job! They didn't need a drummer at the beginning. Yet all that was where I got started.

Buddy [Holly] bought a Stratocaster in 1954, we got together, and, yeah, what's funny is that was the very time when Nanci was being born. But what I love about working on this album, apart from Nanci, who has become a great friend, is working with Jim Rooney. He just gets you to play your drums, no tweaking this, no technical jive. It's like the old days, recording forty years ago. So Jim and Nanci both have that purist kind of approach. And so even though I've played "Walk Right Back" a million times, this was like playing it for a new audience, like being reintroduced to it ourselves.

same song, another voice

JOE B. MAULDIN, BASS

What I still love about "Walk Right Back" is that it has a liveliness to it that really excites me. I know it's been, let's say, a couple of years since we first played it, but even when we're on tour and that intro comes up, I want to start dancing. And I can look back to before the Everly Brothers even heard it, when I told Sonny, "What a tune, man! This is great." And it is.

As for playing bass, I started out looking at someone like Bill Black and thinking, "Man, he sure is playin' the fire out of that stand-up bass. That's what I want to do." And I would do all that slappin' the bass, ridin' the bass, falling back with it, putting on a show. In fact, I probably worked more at puttin' on a show than at learning how to play the bass. Because to tell you the truth, I wouldn't regard myself as the best damn bass player in the world. Only when we started playing with Nanci did I have to start learning how to play the bass. Suddenly I had to listen to the tune and write me a sheet and work on it at home before I went into the studio. But I'll tell you what: I sure do appreciate the perfection she puts into her work. You can hear it on this album.

9

canadian
whiskey

Words and Music by Tom Russell

Joe: *A Tom Russell song and Nanci gets to be Sylvia to Ian Tyson!*

Nanci: Yeah. We brought in Tom's mentor, Ian Tyson, to sing it. And also Andrew Hardin, from Tom Russell's band. But to have Ian Tyson there right in front of me, with our microphones facing each other, and to sing "Canadian Whiskey" was, I imagine, what it would be like for a lot of people if Bob Dylan was standing a foot away from them! And I did get to be Sylvia!

I was only five, six years old when my dad first picked up Ian and Sylvia's records in 1960, 1961. And of course Bill and Bonnie Hearne helped me so much when I was a girl. Theirs was the first band I sang backup for, played and toured with. But more than that, they were such an influence on Texas songwriters because it became your goal in life to have Bill and Bonnie Hearne sing your songs. You knew if they chose your song, you were a real writer, because they never sang anything other than the top songs. They were the best song interpreters in the world. Bill is also the best darn flattop [guitar] player you ever heard, and Bonnie is such a great piano player and has a wonderful voice. They are just the truest heroes you could have, the truest form of purity and innocence. Incredible talent. On their album *Diamonds in the Rough* I sing a duet with Bonnie on "Georgetown," which was

*Tom Russell
and Nanci
Griffith*
DUBLIN,
1997

———

*photo by
Gerry
O'Leary*

151

especially poignant for me because that was a song they recorded right after I had left them to go solo.

As for "Canadian Whiskey," I feel like that woman in the hills of Montana. I don't talk to anybody, I don't go anywhere. Someday I will be that woman out there sipping Canadian whiskey, and I never will speak!

Joe: *I suspect that you are right on that!*

Nanci: I probably am! But I don't feel like I want to be that woman and be that wronged, so that I decide to hide myself away and drink Canadian whiskey and totally ignore the rest of the world. But this is one of my favorite Tom Russell songs.

Joe: *When you choose songs, how deeply do you need to identify with the characters, the narrators?*

Nanci: A whole lot. I always find a character to live within, embody, take over, in music. They always have a place in my heart, though no one will ever really know which character I really related to in "Boots of Spanish Leather." No one will know which one was me because it's all in the first person.

same song, same voice

Another perspective:
Nanci listening to playback

Ian Tyson. What a voice! And even now, listening to his voice, I realize I am probably going to love this album until I die. Just to sing with Ian Tyson is such a moment, it's made me realize that it is a gift for any person to realize what such moments really, really mean. Sometimes things go past and people look back and, with hindsight, say, "Why didn't I enjoy that while it was happening, but then, how could I have known it would turn out to be so special?" But I knew all along how special these recordings were. As a kid, to listen to all these people and then, as an adult, to get to know them and share the making of music with them really is something that probably could be understood only by someone who loves music as much as I do. Listen to that violin part by Fats Kaplin. It really is extraordinary. And Bonnie singing there with Ian Tyson. Pure magic!

same song, another voice

JIM ROONEY

Tom Russell has been a very early and loyal and long supporter of Nanci's, and she has always been a big supporter of his. Tom and Ian Tyson have done a lot of work together, written some good songs together. And Ian and Sylvia were an influential duo, which is shown here in the fact that we did Sylvia's song "You Were on My Mind" and Ian's "Summer Wages." But Ian's voice is a very distinctive voice from the heyday of the folk era. As for the question of what makes a great voice, it's something to do with the personality that comes across. It's immediately identifiable. And the name of this album is *Other Voices*. As people listen to it they are going to hear a lot of personalities coming through. And if the voice is authentic it also captures the soil, the soul of a people, the sense of time and place.

Tom Russell
1996

Bonnie Hearne
NASHVILLE, 1996

"Canadian Whiskey"
photos by Alan Messer

desperadoes
waiting for
a train

Words and Music by Guy Clark

Nanci: Guy Clark is the only person I can listen to sing this whole song right through, as one character. When he sings it, it's this person's life running right by you. Apart from when he performs it, it always seemed like a group thing to me. So with that in mind it became clear that I needed to bring in the whole Texas brat pack, all Guy's friends, to do this. And it was extraordinary to have Eric Taylor there, Steve Earle, Rodney Crowell, Jimmie Dale Gilmore, Jerry Jeff Walker, and Guy Clark. Now, these fellows have all been hanging around, causing trouble, for years, and that's why it seems so fitting to have them singing "Desperadoes Waiting for a Train."

They're so straight now! But they all used to be wild children. And to see Steve Earle and Jerry Jeff get into something of a squabble over what verses they were going to sing was part of it all. They both wanted to be the little sidekick, sing that line, "When I was a kid they all called me Sidekick." And when Jerry Jeff and Steve got into that tussle, Guy intervened and said, "Did anybody ever consider that I might want to sing it myself?" Nobody had even consulted Guy about it! But it ended up that Steve took the first part and Jerry Jeff took

Nanci Griffith
1997

photo by
Señor
McGuire

left to right:

Eric Taylor, Jimmie Dale Gilmore, Steve Earle, Rodney Crowell, Nanci Griffith,
Jerry Jeff Walker, Guy Clark, Jim Rooney

NASHVILLE, 1997

"Desperadoes Waiting for a Train"
photo by Alan Messer

the second, so he won. He had the seniority. But it was brilliant. And when Eric got into it, it was very different, because he's from Georgia, and he's got a southern accent, whereas everybody else was from Texas. And it was really neat to have that different flavor. Then when Guy comes in and I get to sing that last verse with him, it just slays me. This character is my grandfather. He's everybody's grandfather.

Joe: *But that interpretation of "Desperadoes" does sum up how this album, more so than the first, really is almost a rosary of voices, intrinsic to, but set apart from, Nanci Griffith as often as possible. In this song, for example, you move to the fore only on those final lines.*

Nanci: Jim Rooney called the shots on this track, and when they divided it up, they didn't leave me but those two lines to sing! And I wasn't going to get into that squabble about who sings what. But, yes, more often than on the first album I do take a backward step on many of the songs, for the reasons you mention. These songs are intrinsic to my life, but I don't necessarily need to sing them right through. I just need to ensure that they are sung again.

s a m e   s o n g ,   s a m e   v o i c e

A n o t h e r   p e r s p e c t i v e :
N a n c i   l i s t e n i n g   t o   p l a y b a c k

We left in that cough at the beginning because that's a trademark of Guy Clark. He nearly always coughs before he introduces a song, tells a story as a lead-in, whatever. We were going to cut it out, but then we decided not to. Jim and I both agreed that if you are listening to this album on your own, Guy almost scares you when he comes in there, but if you weren't paying attention, you are now! And listen to that line ["taught me how to drive his car"]. Rodney's voice and Jimmie Dale Gilmore's voice back-to-back are really wonderful together. Richard Thompson's electric guitar there also is perfect. So few notes, but it just spits at you, grabs you. [At the line "To a bar they called Green Frog Café"], that's Mr. Earle! Fabulous. [At the line "One day I looked up and he was pushing eighty"], that's Eric. And that's me! I'd been gone so long I wondered would I ever be coming back into the song! But I came in straight after Eric. And at the end of the song we all just held our breath before letting that song go. "Glorious" is the only way to describe Guy's song "Deperadoes Waiting for a Train." A song full of glory.

ꞏꞏ same song, another voice. ꞏꞏ

JIM ROONEY

What we were talking about earlier, different textures and resonances in voices, really comes across in this track. My wife, Carol, was listening to this cut, and she wasn't particularly familiar with the song, though she'd met Guy Clark a couple of times. But she said, "Boy, he seems to have an awful lot of changes in his voice!" I had to tell her there were six people singing! Yet in that shifting from one voice to another you can hear those different personalities come across, though nearly all those singers come from Texas. And there is something about Texas—I don't know what it is—that does something to people's adenoids! Of course, Jerry Jeff Walker is originally from New York State, but he's absorbed a lot of that Texas sound.

One of my favorite things about this cut is Guy Clark's cough! Nanci is right, we did purposely leave that in because it's part of Guy's persona. It's like he clears his throat and he speaks. And then he speaks with great authority. I also did like the idea of having all these other Texas voices around him, to sing this song. But he is very much a leader of that group. And people admire him and admire his writing, because he is a very careful writer. And a very proud writer. Guy is proud of these songs that he comes out with, because he's worked really hard on them. They come out of his life. This a true story about Guy growing up. That's what he made out of his own life. And I think it's a stunning song. I've always thought it was. And I was really pleased to have these other voices sing with him.

ꞏꞏ same song, another voice ꞏꞏ

GUY CLARK, COMPOSER

My favorite version of this song, so far, is Slim Pickens's version, because it is so touching, the way he reads it, doesn't even try to sing. But I must say that

*Jim Rooney, Richard
Thompson, and Doug
Trantow*
LOS ANGELES, 1996

*"Desperadoes Waiting
for a Train"*

Guy Clark
NASHVILLE, 1996

*"Desperadoes Waiting
for a Train"*

*photos by
Alan Messer*

while we were recording this, I thought it was all very chaotic. Y'see, I wrote it as a very personal one-guy song about this old man, and I wasn't sure it was going to work with all these different voices. The old guy was my grandmother's boyfriend. During World War Two my dad was overseas, and this guy was the only male figure around. He was very important in my life. He was a father figure or maybe a grandfather figure. So "Desperadoes Waiting for a Train" was that personal to me, as true a song as I could write.

Anyway, I wasn't sure if this would still come across with so many people singing one piece. But I was pleasantly surprised, very pleased. Because this is a very warm, emotional version of the song.

꞉ same song, another voice ꞉

RODNEY CROWELL, SINGER-SONGWRITER

This was real fun to do, with people like Guy Clark and Steve Earle, because we all kinda crowded Jerry Jeff out. He kept buttin' in, and we all kept pushing him away. But if Nanci told you that the only row in relation to this song was who would be the sidekick, that's not quite my memory of it! My memory is that Jerry Jeff had a pretty good piece, and me and Guy and Steve Earle were going, "Hey, let's steal some of his lines!" Maybe Nanci didn't see that. But we were all standing around one microphone, and Jerry Jeff was over at another mike, so we could secretly plot against him. Let me tell you, Jerry Jeff had a whole lot more of that song before we got ahold of it! We snookered him on a lot of that! But I really think those voices together worked so well on that song. It's like we brought it back to where it belongs. The gravity of that song is such that it's like moving a tree. You gotta uproot it and just start from the base all over again. Though, if you want a version of this with real gravity, check out the Slim Pickens version! It's great. But then, this song can stand up to all kinds of interpretations.

꞉ same song, another voice ꞉

DOUG LANCIO, GUITAR

As a musician I play to the words. I am lyrically led, and "Desperadoes Waiting for a Train" is a perfect example of this kind of playing. I got a kinda deep vibrato heavy sound through the chorus and just used that over and over again. I tried to echo the mental image of the guys in this song. And . . . being three feet away from those five guys singing that song was pretty inspiring. I also wanted to make it sound a little tough, too, with those voices in there. These are tough-sounding voices. They sound a little weary and definitely aged. It was most definitely a matter of trying to rise to the occasion and capture all of that, everything that was going on in the song during the session.

|: s a m e s o n g , a n o t h e r v o i c e :|

ERIC TAYLOR, SINGER-SONGWRITER

There was six or seven of us crowded into a tight circle in a sound booth in Nashville: Guy Clark with his guitar, Nanci to the left of him, then Rodney Crowell, Steve Earle, me, and Jimmie Dale Gilmore to complete the circle. Jerry Jeff Walker sat off to the side with the band because he was also with his guitar. Everybody in the circle was somehow Texas—either born there or had spent so much time there they wouldn't claim any other place.

Nanci dealt out the lines to the song, made some suggestions, lit some candles. We ran through the song, got our parts together, and I think we nailed it next time 'round. Afterwards we all stood around for pictures. Sounds easy. It was, because of the song. Nobody from Texas would dare make that cut a difficulty. Griffith knew what she was doin'. Maybe those nuts are right. Maybe Texas ought to be its own little nation. But then you'd need a passport to go to Tennessee.

11

wings
of a
dove

Words and Music by Bob Ferguson

Joe: *So who the hell is Bob Ferguson?*

Nanci: The person who wrote this song. Nobody I know ever met him. But it was Lucinda Williams's version turned me on to it. She learned it from country singer Ferlin Husky. It evolved that way. I used to sing it with Lucinda late at night. Two daring young women out driving ourselves around America, stupidly, by ourselves, playing music. That's its roots for me. And we recorded it the way we used to sing it, me singing the fifth to Lucinda, and Lee Satterfield, from my Blue Moon Orchestra, singing the third. So it's three-part harmony most of the way, and some of the way it's just Lucinda and me.

Joe: *What attracted you to the song?*

Nanci: When there's so much trouble on this earth, this song is a point of release. It's just a pure Christian gospel song, like "Let Jesus In." It's just such a nice, spiritual thought: "Let nothing trouble thee, let nothing worry thee"—that whole sentiment. "Wings of a Dove" gives you that same sense of peacefulness.

*Nanci Griffith
and
Lucinda
Williams
1993*

---

*photo from
Nanci
Griffith's
personal
collection*

163

‖: s a m e   s o n g ,   s a m e   v o i c e . :‖

A n o t h e r   p e r s p e c t i v e :
N a n c i   l i s t e n i n g   t o   p l a y b a c k

The session for this was wonderful. Lucinda kicked it off with rhythm guitar, and it was as if there wasn't a twenty-two-year gap since we first sang it together. We just sang it like we'd never stopped singing it every night after we finished our work. So we got it in, I think, no more than two takes.

On this one Doug Lancio played a little resonator guitar, kinda sounds like a Dobro. And he just amazes me because he'd just picked that up in the last year to go with this type of material.

‖: s a m e   s o n g ,   a n o t h e r   v o i c e :‖

JIM ROONEY

This was a very popular song in the sixties when Ferlin Husky had a big hit with it. But in this version . . . Lucinda and Nanci were going back to their start, when they were playing in coffeehouses and sang this song together. And it's a song I remember singing up in Cambridge, at a coffeehouse. I guess I learned it off a Ferlin Husky record, but it seemed to seep into the culture very quickly. So many people used to sing this song in coffeehouses. And the feeling of Nanci and Lucinda singing this together, back when they were young girls is part of what we tried to recapture on this recording. Nanci wanted to hold some of that feeling, bring it to this interpretation of "Wings of a Dove." And there is a sweetness about this recording, which I love. We kept it as simple as possible, though I do love what James Hooker played on this—the chimey keyboard thing, which is kind of eerie. And I love, also, Lee Satterfield's vocal. I just thought this was a pure performance overall. Lovely stuff.

‖: s a m e   s o n g ,   a n o t h e r   v o i c e :‖

LUCINDA WILLIAMS, SINGER-SONGWRITER

Nanci first approached me about this one night when we were over at John Prine's house talking about old times. Somehow we burst into song, and

nanci griffith's other voices

164

even that night we ended up singing "Wings of a Dove."

This song has been a part of my musical history since I was a child. Y'see, both my grandfathers were Methodist ministers, so I grew up hearing a lot of these old hymns, and somehow "Wings of a Dove" got into my life at that level. And I do believe in the sentiments in the song, though not in the traditional religious sense. I think it speaks in other ways. It's not just a basic Christian thing. [*She sings*]: "On the wings of a snow white dove." See? It just feels so good to sing. Even singing just that image: "Snow white dove." And also: "He sends his pure, sweet love." To me it's just about love, sending out a message of love and the "he" isn't necessarily Jesus. You can interpret it your own way. It doesn't have to be taken literally.

I've always sung that type of song. And I was raised in a very non-traditional environment. I went to the Unitarian Church, and my father was an agnostic, so this hung a question mark over all the rest of this stuff. But that doesn't mean I could sing songs like "Will the Circle Be Unbroken?" and "Gray Speckled Bird" and not believe in them. They're beautiful songs, regardless of how you interpret the religious aspect. But there is this whole [issue] of spirituality versus religion. And I interpret these songs more from the purely spiritual point of view in a nondenominational sense. And what is ironic is that, despite all the churches and so on in Nashville, there is a spiritual void here. But you can't feel connected in that way, necessarily. At least I don't. Apart from when I sing a song like "Wings of a Dove." I tune in to that force.

Joe Jackson and
Lucinda Williams
SPRING 1997

photo by
Alan Messer

12

dress of
laces

Words and Music by John Grimaudo and Steve Puntenney
(a.k.a. Saylor White)

Joe: *Another tragic song, Nanci.*

Nanci: It is, isn't it. The girl has been abused so much all her life that she ends up shooting the wrong man. Pure tragedy, like an old Irish traditional ballad. It sounds like it was written in the 1800s, but it's a contemporary song. The co-writer of this song, Steve Puntenney, I didn't know. But John Grimaudo was a dear friend of Eric Taylor and myself when we were married, in the late seventies and early eighties. And Eric, Lyle Lovett, and I used to sing "Dress of Laces" together at John Grimaudo's. We never even knew there was a co-writer until we recorded it this time.

All three of us had individual versions of this song, so I went back to the source—Grimaudo—and did it that way. It's a beautiful story, a heartbreaking story, a song I love because it has a great story line to it. It's the little masterpiece on this record, mostly because voices were reunited on this song that haven't sung together in so long. Lyle and I haven't recorded together since 1982, so all that was very special to us.

Lyle is such a huge fan of Eric's and would come around to the house at the time when he was a journalist. He got an interview with me to get into the house to pay his regards to

Nanci Griffith
and Lyle Lovett
N A S H V I L L E ,
1 9 9 6

"Dress of Laces"
photo by
Alan Messer

167

Eric! The first couple of times he would leave and Eric would say, "I've asked you not to bring people you don't know into the house," and it was like my father speaking to me! Anyway, they became close and Eric was an influence on Lyle's style. You can hear it. Listen to Eric Taylor's records and you'll hear Lyle Lovett.

And also, what I love about "Dress of Laces" is the string arrangement, which I did. The cellists are Ron de la Vega [from the Blue Moon Orchestra] and John Ketchins, who has worked with me since 1983 on every album except *Late Night Grande Hotel*. I had this chart in mind because I'm a real cello person. I like big, strong pizzicato, and I really wanted teardrops here, just like they were there in Buddy Holly's song "Raining in My Heart."

Joe: *On a more personal level, have you and Eric Taylor stayed in touch after the breakup of your marriage, or do you both just meet on occasions like this? Have you remained friends?*

Nanci: Yes. We are friends. In fact I think we are a true example of people who can be friends after a marriage breakup. There doesn't have to be any ugliness, even though you may feel that hatred, which everybody is going to feel in the immediate aftermath of the breakup, because love does turn immediately to hate. All that remembered passion becomes hatred. But it is

only for a brief moment. And you have to remember that you once loved and respected each other. So much so that there is always that lingering feeling there, that lingering tension.

Eric sat in with us during an outdoor festival last year, and his wife, Martha, and I are dear, dear friends. But at one point Martha had gone to park the car and there was this huge storm, so everything got shut down.

Eric Taylor, outside Jack's Tracks Studio
Nashville, November 1996

photo by Alan Messer

Later they're running to their car and Martha can't remember where she parked it, and it's hailing on them. Eric turns to her and says, "All right, Nanci, what the hell did you do with the damn car?" Martha just stops in the hail and says, "I'm gonna tell you one more time: 'My name is Martha!'" He didn't blink an eye. He just said, "It's all right. Anytime anything irritates me, that's the first name that comes into my head." And J. I. Allison, who was with me, said, "That is the quickest thinking I have ever heard, on any man's part. You know he's a psychologist when he can dig himself out of that one!"

‖: s a m e   s o n g ,   a n o t h e r   v o i c e :‖

JIM ROONEY

This is a gorgeous song, and I love Nanci's warmth in this song, the quality of her voice. The quality of the three voices in this song is heartbreaking. Nanci, Eric, and Lyle get what the song is about, absolutely. They all have such a long history. And that too comes across.

‖: s a m e   s o n g ,   a n o t h e r   v o i c e :‖

STEVE PUNTENNEY,
A.K.A. SAYLOR WHITE, COMPOSER

I taught this song to John Grimaudo in 1976 and never expected it to go any further than that. Luckily, John kept playing the song and, along the way, added a verse and used his remarkable guitar-playing talent to create a very nice song. John was the musical mule who carried the song around for years until Nanci chose to record it.

Songs seem to have a life of their own, and it is our good fortune to have Nanci, Eric, and Lyle plant this song in the great American musical garden. In my opinion, they gave us a wonderful performance.

As far as the song itself goes, being asked how we could write a "woman's song" was a nice compliment. In truth, I can't answer that question. If what we wrote touched on certain aspects of being female, then, in a larger sense, I think such tales comment on the more tragic nuances of being human.

If I am honest, I am not sure that I have ever written a song. More often than not it is as if I just wrote it down. I am not talking about channeling or claiming divine inspiration. I heard this song as clearly as I heard

John Grimaudo
ANDERSON FAIR

photo by Bob Johnston

Saylor White,
NASHVILLE, 1996

"Dress of Laces"

photo from Saylor White's personal collection

the sound of the wind. I just wrote what I heard. And I believe that this song, like many others, would have been written by someone else had I not been dutiful in playing scribe to the muse. I think the scribes outnumber the muses, and I feel fortunate to have been in the right place at the right time with my antenna tuned to the right station to hear this song. So I am honored to have this song interpreted and recorded by all those who participated in its coming to fruition.

13

summer
wages

Words and Music by Ian Tyson

Joe: *Why does Ian Tyson's "Summer Wages" mean so much to you?*

Nanci: Ian Tyson just had a way with songs like this. The beauty of the way he talks about the mining camps, the lumber, and the sailors. You have this whole picture of Vancouver and the western seaboard. Its images were foreign for me, growing up in Texas, having never been across the Red River much less western Canada until I was in my twenties.

The image of the dealer always fascinated me; it's something like the "Wall of Death" motif. So the song just has meant that much to me over the years, and that's why you hear my voice crack at the end when I sing the repeat on "and never hit seventeen"—as in "If you play against the dealer, because you know the odds won't ride with you."

For these sessions Tom Russell came in to sing Ian's part, and as you know, Ian Tyson is his mentor. And Carolyn Hester sang the harmony on the choruses. It was so much fun. Ian was there, too, and he's such a massive hero of mine. But he is real strict about interpretation. He doesn't want his lyrics changed. Tom had changed a lyric as a result of years of singing the song on his own. It was just one line about "my city shoes, which I swore I would never wear again." And Ian

Nanci Griffith
1997

photo by
Señor
McGuire

Ian Tyson
NASHVILLE, 1996

Songwriter:
"Summer Wages"
Vocalist:
"Canadian Whiskey"

Bela Fleck
1997

During the sessions for
"Summer Wages"

Fats Kaplin
NASHVILLE, 1996

Playing on "Summer Wages"
photos by
Alan Messer

came in and said, "It's 'I swore I would never *do* again,' not 'never *wear* again.'" But Tom just never did change it. And it was like father and son, an obstinacy there, and neither would give way. So unless Ian was going to take the microphone away from Tom, there was no way he was going to change that lyric. But it meant the same thing, whatever way he sang it, so we did it anyway.

||: s a m e   s o n g ,   s a m e   v o i c e :||

Another perspective:
Nanci listening to the playback

That opening verse of "Summer Wages," to me, contains some of the greatest lines ever written. In fact, until now I hadn't realized that that line about the dealer could apply to drug addicts, particularly [addicts] who are seventeen years old. . . . And Carolyn got a great kick out of that line: "And the hookers standing watchfully, waiting by the door!" She loved singing that line!

||: s a m e   s o n g ,   a n o t h e r   v o i c e :||

JIM ROONEY

This is a classic song, one of the big songs of the folk revival, but it's a difficult song to cover, because Tom Russell's performance is so well known.

As for "Summer Wages" itself, I'm not sure what, exactly, it was that people hooked into. I guess it was the idea that you can have life, love, and money but then, in a moment, it's all gone. And the idea of summer wages, for those of us who grew up in the suburbs, is kind of an exotic concept. But even so, people seem to instinctively understand the song. It's just a beautifully written piece of work.

14

he was a
friend of mine

Traditional, Arranged by Dave Van Ronk and Eric Von Schmidt

Joe: *Why did you choose to record Van Ronk's classic?*

Nanci: Just as my dad wore out the Weavers' record of "Wimoweh," he also wore out the record of Dave Van Ronk's "He Was a Friend of Mine." And we were talking earlier about how Eric and I remained friends. Well, in that sense it's appropriate that he should come in and sing on "He Was a Friend of Mine." He also admired Dave Van Ronk and always wanted to work with him. And their two voices together are lovely. So you have those two voices, along with the beautiful combination of Rosalie Sorrels and Odetta and Jean Ritchie and Lucy Kaplansky, then all these backing vocals that come in at the end, like Julie Gold and everyone who was in the studio! For me it was not only a revisitation to all those times I heard that song in my house, but it's also a traditional song. It's a Library of Congress song; the original composer is unknown. All I know is that it was the essential Dave Van Ronk. And it was such a visitation to that.

Nanci Griffith
NEW YORK,
1996

"He Was a Friend of Mine"

photo by Alan Messer

Dave Van Ronk
NEW YORK, 1996

"He Was a Friend of Mine"

left to right:
Doug Lancio, Caitlin Von
Schmidt, Eric Von Schmidt
(seated), Rosalie Sorrels,
Jean Ritchie,
Lucy Kaplansky, Julie Gold,
Frank Christian, Eric Taylor
NEW YORK, 1996

"He Was a Friend
of Mine"

photos by Alan Messer

‖: s a m e   s o n g ,   s a m e   v o i c e :‖

Another perspective:
Nanci listening to playback

Everybody agrees that recording this song was the most fun. The blend of the voices is so otherworldly; it's like it could have been recorded seventy years ago. There's Jean Ritchie doing that really high voice and Dave Van Ronk just below her. And Nina Gerber's guitar playing is just incredible. She and Frank Christian together are just . . . boy, what a combination! You can just hear people doing their own version of the verses in this at parties.

‖: s a m e   s o n g ,   a n o t h e r   v o i c e . :‖

JIM ROONEY

I've known this song for a long, long time. I learned it from my friend Eric Von Schmidt, who learned it from a Library of Congress recording at around the same time Dave Van Ronk recorded it. But Dave's version has a different feel to it, and this was the version Nanci learned. Dave's version is jazzier. He finger-picks it, and it has jazzier chords. Eric's is more country blues, a little simpler, musically. But Nanci learned it from Dave's version, so that's the one we did.

That New York base to the folk revival meant a lot to Nanci, because she got involved with Rosalie Sorrels, who lived in Saratoga Springs and was an early role model for Nanci. Then through Frank Christian, she became acquainted with the New York folk scene. Of course, Van Ronk is a major figure in that scene. And Jean Ritchie, although she's from Kentucky, also lived for many years in that area. Nanci associates Jean with the early folk revival. So this song was an opportunity to bring all these people together.

Doug Lancio and Frank Christian

NEW YORK, 1996

photo by Alan Messer

| : | same song, another voice | : |

NINA GERBER, GUITARIST

It was an honor for me to be included in these projects. It's a Who's Who of legends, heroes, legends-to-be, and amazing musicians who have inspired me as well.

The *Other Voices* projects are a great lesson in the importance of keeping the music that we care about alive. If everybody sings only their own songs, who will play the music that has inspired and taught us? For Nanci Griffith, one of the finest songwriters of our time, to have dedicated two of her albums to pay tribute to the music and people that have influenced her says so much. It is a passionate dedication to music and to the souls it feeds. Truly a class act.

‖: s a m e   s o n g ,   a n o t h e r   v o i c e :‖

D AVE V AN R ONK ,
ARRANGER, VOCALIST, GUITARIST

On the morning of the session for "He Was a Friend of Mine," I had just completed the last leg of a three-day drive back to New York from a two-week tour, appropriately enough, of Texas, and "tired" isn't the word for it. But as soon as I walked into that studio and saw who all was there, I was up and running as if I had just gotten back from a vacation. Old home week: Jean Ritchie, Frank Christian, Odetta, Rosalie, Eric, and of course, Nanci herself. Family jokes and lots of gossip. And when the music began, it was like a community sing with a choir of angels—I knew I was really home.

15

interlude:
odetta

Joe: *Nanci claims that "Wimoweh" "says it all" for her in relation to the way you led all the people into the fold during the recording saying "Let's do all this together," and she suggests that sums up her hopes for these albums: that they will lead the general public back to folk music, "the most neglected roots music in America."*

Odetta: She's certainly doing her part for it, isn't she? And the point is that except for erudite musicologists, for a very long time we in this country didn't know we had a folk music of our own. We felt it either had to be from England or Europe, but God bless all those men and women who originally collected our own folk songs, songs of everyday people all over America.

But until then we really were so conscious of the fact that we didn't have any culture, at least according to whoever was writing the history books. So in the thirties, as the union movement began, people realized they weren't too far away from where the music had started, and they used it to propagandize and to bring all these spirits together in song and help those spirits up. Then, coming into the civil rights movement and the anti–Vietnam War movement there was a continuation of that. But in the sixties, the fickle eye of the industry saw that many people were coming to folk concerts, getting up and singing together, and there was a lot of energy around. And it was good, positive political energy.

Odetta
Courtesy of
Douglas A.
Yaeger
Productions

So folk music has always been part of causes that were helpful to people, over, under, around, and right through the good fight, whatever it was for. That to me is what folk music is all about. And this is what Nanci is doing her best to carry on, I believe, this very real history of the people in the United States.

Joe: *In that you mean all creeds and colors. You're not limiting such comments to any particular ethnic group, are you?*

Odetta: I myself am saying all creeds and colors. There might be some who only consider folk music in this country to be music from Appalachia or wherever. But that's their hang-up.

Joe: *But didn't that happen in the sixties too, when schisms appeared in the civil rights movement and the more radical African Americans told Pete Seeger, for example, that as a white person his contribution to the struggle was no longer needed? This understandably added to his own confusion, sense of rejection, and made him raise some serious questions about the civil rights movement and the role music played in that process.*

Odetta: I can see that it would. But I never heard that side of the story and it certainly never was part of my experience.

Joe: *Any experience of, again, as happened with Pete, someone like Lillian Hellman describing songs such as "We Shall Overcome" as namby-pamby and politically naive?*

Odetta: I'm not sure that whatever she was writing at the time did more than what Pete Seeger did when he lifted people's spirits when he got them singing.

There are too many times when people get a leg up by pulling someone else down. Within this country, every last one of us has a bias, prejudice ingrained in our bones. That's the country we grew up in. Nobody specifically was teaching it to us, that's just the way the land lay. So there are people who do not believe they are biased or prejudiced or racist because it hasn't been demonstrated to them. I remember a time when even Pete was not as enlightened as he is today. All of us had to grow. Our consciousness was being raised throughout all that time, more information was coming in.

Joe: *But at that point were you all as one?*

Odetta: No. We agreed on points, but we might not have agreed on how to get there. But then as soon as you add the music it is something else, quite unlike a sermon. It's another level of vibration that you are sharing here, that healing stuff.

Joe: *So you probably agree with Nanci who sees music this way, says she loves poet Seamus Heaney's line about how poetry, or by extension song, should put a tongue to people's silence?*

Odetta: I know of Seamus Heaney. Isn't that a lovely line? And yes, so true.

Joe: *Well, in the book, Nanci also says that people like you and Leadbelly and Guthrie, in effect, put a tongue to silence in America and defined the American psyche as much as Henry Ford or Martin Luther King Jr.*

Odetta: Isn't that something? [*Laughs.*]

Joe: *But do you accept such claims to be true or more hero worship on her part?*

Odetta: I can receive what she's saying but I don't know what is in anybody else's mind or how they respond. But I can believe in what they say, that it is true for them. And it honors me, compliments me, takes me beyond the area of luxury tax!

Joe: *She also says that before the recording of "Wimoweh" you were very much determined to point out what the song was really about, like people's freedom.*

Odetta: That is important to me. Nanci also has that sense of where words come from and what they mean. I've not heard everything she's done but I notice that in the music she picks to do, there are significant words involved. I needed to point that out during the recording session for "Wimoweh."

And I remember, too, back when Johnny Cash was doing his television show from the Grand Ole Opry he invited me to appear with him. But for the finale they wanted to do, y'know that song, "I got shoes, you got shoes, all God's children got shoes," and I had to say, "Excuse me, I cannot do that song because all God's children don't got shoes."

Joe: *And how did Johnny Cash respond to that?*

Odetta: Very well indeed! And we went out finding another song we could all do together. But we certainly didn't do "All God's Children Got Shoes." And sometimes all it takes is for someone to say "I don't like singing this because" and to explain the "because." But a lot of the time people don't really express what they are feeling. When I was growing up we never did. We're only in that age now. That's another area where we have grown tremendously. We're finding ways to say what it is that we think and feel.

Joe: *You mean in song, at this fundamental human level, as opposed to simply in a political sense?*

Odetta: Yes. And I'm often asked, "How was it in the sixties?" and I say, "We sang together." I was a hermit back then; I didn't hang out with a lot of people, a lot of packs. So my relationships were that we didn't really sit and talk politics because the idea was, "Since you sang the song I agree with, you must agree with me!" The politics often weren't an issue.

Joe: *In the book, Nanci also says, "Odetta taught us the meaning of soul, and when she comes in (when you hear her sing), you just say, 'Bless you.'" That kind of says it all, too, doesn't it?*

Odetta: That, too, is wonderful of her to say, but again, I can't take credit for that! All I can say is that when I sing I am still trying to lift people's spirits. The thing to do is to devote yourself totally to the song you are doing, not singing it the way you think somebody else wants to hear it but through your own experience, whatever.

Performers are some of the biggest gamblers on the planet. What's the guarantee that somebody is going to like what you are doing? So you put your faith out there, on the line, and operate according to the hope that somebody will like it. Or at least not boo you off the stage! So when you give what's inside you to give, you are the only one on the face of the earth that can give what it is you've got to give! And if you do that as honestly as possible, you give people something to respond to. That to me is what singing is all about. And some, yes, do call this soul.

And the best thing about Nanci's involvement in all this is that audiences for this music are growing. So in that sense whether it is through her, me, or those of us who are involved in these albums and this book, we are bringing the music back to the people.

Joe: *As in the recording of "Wasn't That a Mighty Storm"?*

Odetta: Definitely. Recording that song I was totally involved in the energy and the spirit of it all. And that does very much capture all of what you and I have been talking about today.

But what I would want to do with a song is often something that I become aware of *after* the song is sung. Again, as I say, if you're worried about how the song will be received, you're living in the future, nervous over something that hasn't happened yet. So what you have to do is live the moment, appreciate and enjoy that moment you are in, and give everything to that moment. Much the same as it is in relation to life itself. That's when something does become spiritually uplifting for all involved. I hope that is true of our recording of "Wasn't That a Mighty Storm" and this book.

16

hard times
come again
no more

Words and Music by Stephen Collins Foster

Joe: *Tell me some more about why you didn't like what had been done to this song over time? What prompted you to go back to the original sheet music?*

Nanci: I've always been a big fan of Stephen Foster, because I grew up with my father's Stephen Foster songbooks. One contained his songs written in shape note, which is something the Welsh started. Stephen Foster was also such a major influence on all American music, from pop to blues to jazz, everything. This song has been adapted to suit all those genres and he passed on all these musical traditions and combined them. For example, he took all those influences from the black gospel music he listened to, the traditional music his family brought from Belfast, plus the black field songs and the European tradition. All of that he brought together to create this entity of Stephen Foster material, which is so enormous. And he brought together all those

*Nanci Griffith
and Peaches*
1996

Recording session for Other
Voices, Too

*photo by
Alan Messer*

black and white influences long before Louis Armstrong, jazz, and of course rhythm and blues or rock and roll. He did all this before the Civil War! He was the first to integrate these forms, racially, culturally, and ethnically.

He was also a man who fought, throughout his life, for the rights of the writer. And at that particular time in history, you learned to play the song from sheet music. So in those days, just as today we run out to buy the latest albums by our favorite singer-songwriters, back then people ran out and bought the sheet music of Stephen Foster's latest song. I've been reading biographies of Stephen Foster since I was a child, so I've always been well aware of who he was, what he did, and what he meant to writers, especially in terms of his position on copyright, which was his belief that you cannot own someone else's art.

The Library of Congress in America set up the concept of copyright ownership largely because there were so many people out there forging songs like "Oh, Susannah." Foster's legal case was against a specific sheet-music manufacturer who was bootlegging the sheet music. Foster fought that battle throughout his life, and thanks to him, we have laws that protect writers against theft and plagiarism.

Joe: *So do you regard Stephen Foster as the father of popular music in America, and, by extension, throughout the world?*

Nanci: I would say so, yes. For example, the similarities between Stephen Foster and Jimmy Webb are enormous. Likewise Harlan Howard, who is my great mentor and who became the father figure in my life after I left home to become a songwriter. In fact, when I first moved to Nashville, he took me past a housing area that is funded by charities called Stephen Foster Homes, which are flats for elderly people. And he told me about Bardstown, where the Stephen Foster museum is, the archive is, where you can go and touch the real sheet music that Stephen wrote himself. Foster was a massive influence on pop and on songwriters. He started the ball rolling by initiating that fight for copyright royalties. So he definitely was the father of American music in many ways.

Joe: *But hasn't it been said of Stephen Foster that, like white musicians during the Jazz Age and white rockers in the 1950s, he just ripped off black culture and gave neither credit nor money back to those people?*

Nanci: I don't think so. He lived in a black community in Kentucky and never had slaves of his own. Basically he was the Bob Dylan of his day, and he sang of their lives and gave it to us in reality. And nothing was spared. So it wasn't cultural appropriation.

Joe: *It could also be argued that American popular music, like jazz and rock and roll, was the result of a synthesis of black and white culture, the by-product of the points at which they met, rather than "owned" exclusively by either race.*

Nanci: That is how I would see it, yes. Especially in terms of the European traditions that came out of classical music, operetta, music hall, Broadway, and all that.

Joe: *To stay with the race issue for a moment, would you have originally realized that true folk music stems as much from the culture of black musicians like Odetta and Big Bill Broonzy as it does from the landscape inhabited by people like Pete Seeger?*

Nanci: Very much so. After all, Odetta was very much a protégée of Leadbelly. He was a father figure to her. Odetta is next in line to Leadbelly.

Joe: *But in folk culture don't you more often see Woody Guthrie get credit than, say, Leadbelly?*

Nanci: That is true. But I don't think it has to do with race as much as the volume of work. As a young girl I was really fortunate to see Lightnin' Hopkins live and to see Big Mama Thornton many, many times. I certainly never saw any racial divide in terms of folk music. Nor did my family. Folk music always was a multicultural form of expression, as far as we were concerned. And country blues, or Delta blues, was much the same to me—as in the type of music Leadbelly played and people like Woody Guthrie, Lightnin' Hopkins, and Mance Lipscomb carried on, and Willie McTell, Robert Johnson, all those performers I loved.

Joe: *Let's extend this discussion of the roots of American folk music to another "room" that is rarely mentioned. Isn't it true that Native American culture also forms a spiritual base in this music? Indeed, people like Johnny Cash and*

Willie Nelson, whom we regard as grand masters of country music, would probably argue that the real grand masters are the Native Americans. Cash once told me he believes that there will always be a spiritual void at the center of the American psyche until it recognizes that fact. If this is true, why is it that we so rarely see American folk culture celebrated at that level—not even, it must be said, on an album like Other Voices, Other Rooms.

Nanci: I agree with everything you are saying here. Yet something I realized about these albums is that you can't cover all bases. I had covered the plight of Native Americans in my *One Fair Summer's Evening* live album. I did Eric Taylor's "Deadwood, South Dakota, 1877," and that really captured my sentiments about this subject. It says that the white man did take the land away from the Indians and killed their people, jailed them, put them on reservations, and we have to live with that on our conscience, though it's not something we face every day. But it is seen as part of the American folk music landscape, with people like your friend Bill Miller, whose music you have praised publicly along these lines. Quite rightly. And I always felt that Bill has the capacity to pass on what Native Indian folk culture really is, in terms of the music. He does that, in a more authentic fashion, as opposed to Nanci Griffith writing about why Leonard Peltier should be released from prison.

During the saga of Wounded Knee, when the protests were going on, there was so much bad feeling between law enforcement agencies and the Indians on the reservations in Pine Ridge, South Dakota. At one point two FBI agents came onto the reservations without warrants, which is like entering another country without a visa. They got into a shoot-out and were killed, and it was claimed that Leonard Peltier was responsible. It was also proven that he was not there, but he was still sent to prison.

That's been going on now for twenty years, and they should let Leonard out. Investigative journalists have gone in and proved that Leonard didn't do it, but our presidents are so afraid of being politically incorrect on either side of the fence that they keep forgetting to pardon Leonard Peltier. But there are some folk performers who highlight these things, like Bill Miller and Michael Martin Murphy. Michael has always written about Native American concerns, with songs like "Geronimo's Cadillac." That song is about white Americans trying to erase the Native American culture and force them to conform to the white man's culture:

Mary Custy
DUBLIN, 1996

"Hard Times Come Again
No More"
photo by
Gerry O'Leary

Lucy Kaplansky
NEW YORK, 1996

Overdub for "Hard Times
Come Again No More"
photo by Alan
Messer

They put Geronimo in jail down south
So he couldn't look the gift horse in the mouth.
They stole his land, now they'll never give it back,
And they sent Geronimo a Cadillac.

So, as I say, my ex-husband, Eric, wrote about the plight of Native Americans. And now he's written a one-man play based on his songs "I Hear Nevada" and "Joseph Cross." June Tabor recorded "Joseph Cross" on her *Tiger Eyes* album. It's about a turn-of-the-century gunfighter whose 1919 death was surrounded in mystery of a spiritual nature.

I must admit, though, that as a child I wasn't aware that this was part of our folk culture. I didn't even know about Native Americans. You didn't see them in Texas, because most of them were moved to Oklahoma, which is where the larger reservation is.

Joe: *So do you agree that the denial of Native American culture is a hollow in the soul of American folk music in general and, by extension, in rock and roll? In fact, Robbie Robertson recently said, when he brought out his album,* Music for Native Americans, *that he hadn't realized until then that even the Band's music was lacking in this respect. The Band was supposed to represent the definitive return to America's roots, in a musical context. There also is the fact that the so-called King of Rock and Roll, Elvis, was part Native American, though very few commentators refer to that fact.*

Nanci: Again, I agree wholeheartedly with all of that, but the point is that this denial doesn't exist only in American folk music or rock music. It's there in education, at the roots of our culture. I know this because I was a teacher. Children are taught in schools that in 1920 women got the right to vote. They are not told that just four years later, Native Americans also got the right to vote. And that up till then Native Americans were literally prisoners on reservation camps. So if we're denying our history at that level, how could the same level of denial not filter through into our culture in general, including American music? And yes, that is something that needs to be addressed.

Joe: *Let's get back to the roots of the Griffith family. Your grandfather's grandfather emigrated to America around the same time Stephen Foster was writing songs like "Hard Times"?*

Nanci: Yes. He emigrated from Wales in 1857, and he was so dirt-poor that he joined the British army. That was his way out of the poverty in Wales at the same time as the potato famine in Ireland. So the British sent him to Nova Scotia to help with the overwhelming Irish emigration there. Finally he came to the conclusion that he'd just left all that poverty and death behind and didn't want to be reminded of it. So he hopped across the border to America, and at about that time the Civil War started. He was immediately inducted into the Union army. And the Union army put him on a boat to attack the port of Galveston, in Texas, which was still held by the Confederacy. But the northerners lost that battle, and he was arrested. Of course, the British were funding the Confederates, and when they discovered he was a deserter from the British army, they put him in jail! Isn't that wild? Doesn't it really ask the definitive question of how many times can a man be caught? And all of that is part of my history. My folk history, I guess.

same song, same voice

Another perspective:
Nanci listening to playback

I can just see those images in my mind because this song is so beautifully written: "There's a pale sorrowed maiden who toils her life away with a worn heart. . . . There's a song that will linger forever in our ears." And what you describe as my "strange accent" on the word "linger" really was unconscious. But if I am singing well, it's because all these songs are so emotion-packed, like a second skin. They are so effortless to sing. As a singer you do have a responsibility to live up to the songs, not to let down the writers, the musicians, the history of the songs, everything. And the atmosphere that Sharon, Nollaig, and Mary created really was so moving.

Yet I have to say that you wouldn't hear my voice break if we had known, at the time of recording that song, that it was based on the Dickens novel *Hard Times*. I had been told [that the song] was about the Irish famine, and everyone in the studio that day was thinking of that when we recorded the song, especially, obviously,

Dublin Musicians

front row seated: Dolores Keane, Nanci Griffith, Mary Custy, Iain Matthews
back row standing: Adrian Cunningham, Sharon Shannon, Brian
Willoughby, Brian Masterson, Jim Rooney, Pat McInerney, James Hooker, Ron de la
Vega, (Bruce Pearson in background), Nollaig Casey, Doug Lancio, Clive Gregson

photo by Gerry O'Leary

someone like Dolores. So even if that turns out not to have been Stephen Foster's inspiration for the original song, the idea of the famine and the suffering of millions of Irish people definitely was on our minds when we recorded "Hard Times Come Again No More." And in our hearts. That's what you hear in this song. It's definitely what you hear in my voice.

same song, another voice

JIM ROONEY

This song has been done by a lot of people, and I loved a lot of the performances, and maybe I'm prejudiced here, but I *really* love this performance. This was the song we started with, in Dublin. Dolores Keane is a very special person, and I love what she brings to this song.

There is a certain amount of pain in Dolores, and it's the pain of woman. Maybe this is a lot of bullshit, but that's definitely what I hear when Dolores Keane sings. And I think that's why a lot of people respond to her. There's something in there that she can communicate that really touches people deeply. Nanci had it in her mind from the very beginning that Dolores would sing that part in this song. And as Nanci says, it *is* heartbreaking when she comes in. I love the playing of the song, the whole atmosphere of it. And . . . her Irish accent dominates this recording. That's why we wanted to record the song in Dublin, with these players. That gave the song something that I hadn't gotten out of it before. And I know that Nanci was very moved by the music and by Dolores.

Nanci's performance is something I don't think even she herself knew was there, before she did it. It was very moving. Y'know, there aren't too many times when you actually can say you were deeply moved at the moment when you were making the record. The atmosphere in a studio usually goes against that. But this was definitely one of those times. And because this was the first thing we did in Dublin, it gave us a lot of confidence, in terms of knowing that what we were doing was right and had to be done.

PAT MCINERNEY

There were a lot of players on this recording, and we had to keep the pulse of that, because there was so much going on. And I wanted the minstrel feel, like a riverboat, so I played that press roll on the snare, and that moved it along. And I knew we wouldn't have many shots at it, because all of these songs are basically first and second takes. But above all, I really didn't want that pace to get away from us. Usually I just play to Nanci's tempo, because she has a great rhythm sense. But on this album she didn't play as much guitar as usual and even said to me, "You are my rhythm guitar on this," which was a really great compliment, a lovely thing for her to say, and I appreciate that so much.

JOHN MOCK, TIN WHISTLE

I recorded my part as an overdub here in Nashville. And the minute I listened to the tape I knew it was something really special. I've been a big fan of Nanci's for a long time, so that in itself was a big deal. But I'm also into Celtic music, and there are other people on that cut, like Dolores Keane and Sharon Shannon, I'm so pleased to be working with.

As for the song, Stephen Foster's work has been done so much—often badly—that you do lose sight of how great he was. Then you hear it in its original version and go, "Wow!" When I got the tape, as I say, it felt really magical, just sitting at home, working my lines.

So I wrote out a chord chart and kept improvising. And as I'd find bits I liked, I'd write them down, so that, by the end, the blend was working from the chart and improvising off that. Sometimes there'd be a place where the fiddle would play something really beautiful, and I'd write out what she [Nollaig Casey] played and double that line in unison. That, to me, is a big part of Celtic music. Being able to do that is also one of the nice things about doing an overdub. Okay, you miss the joy of being at the actual session, but then, listening later, you can hear something like that fiddle part and arrange your overdub to go with it. In the studio, you wouldn't really have had time to figure out what they were doing and to double all the inflections. Likewise, there might be a line, say, that Philip Donnelly played on the acoustic guitar, earlier on in the song, and you listen to that, keep playing it, then later, as the verse goes into the chorus, you can answer that same line. That can be great fun, and it gives continuity to a song.

same song, another voice

M ATTHEW   R YAN ,   SINGER-SONGWRITER

Hearing Nanci do "Hard Times Come Again No More" made the song blindingly clear to me. I heard Dylan's version and didn't get it. But the pain in Nanci's voice is so sublime. She just makes you feel every word. Sure, I'd prefer if Nanci was a well-adjusted, completely happy person, not prone to depression or whatever, but this proves that the pain in her voice isn't forced, isn't faked. It's a soul thing. Her pain is true, and that's what makes songs like this really breathe. It's hard to listen to and not shiver. Some people just carry a torch for the longest possible time, and Nanci is one of those people. But the way she's burning up, before our eyes, or ears, really is what imbues the music, as far as I'm concerned. And the same is true of the best work done by Leonard Cohen and Bob Dylan, who are the two greatest songwriters and singers of our time, in my opinion. Nanci is driven by the same forces that fire such people. And it all comes across in a song like "Hard Times Come Again No More." The song *is* the soul.

17

wasn't that
a mighty storm

Traditional, Arranged by Tom Rush and Eric Von Schmidt

Joe: *This is the Cecil B. DeMille approach to folk music—a cast of thousands!*

Nanci: Yeah, where the headphones come off and Peaches, my dog, goes and hides underneath the B-3 organ! But this is the "Wimoweh" of *Other Voices, Too,* because it was all done at one time and there were no overdubs.

Basically, this recording means so much to me because the song itself means a lot to me. I've got books on the mighty storm that came through Galveston in 1900, CDs that are narratives, recordings of survivors. Even so, no one knows who wrote this song.

Tom Rush recorded it several times, but the live version on his 1982 *New Year's Eve—Live at Symphony Hall* was my inspiration. It's always the finale of Tom's concerts. And without Tom Rush we would never have heard of Joni Mitchell, Jackson Browne, and so on. Or at least we wouldn't have heard people like Jackson Browne so early on. He was the first one to record so many writers' music. And he's a great writer himself; he wrote "No Regrets." And he found this particular song, "Wasn't That a Mighty Storm" in the Library of Congress.

It has so much personal meaning for me because so much

Nanci Griffith
1997

photo by
Señor
McGuire

201

left to right: Mark Miller (engineer, seated), Carolyn Hester, Maura Kennedy, Tom Rush and his wife, Renée (seated), Jim Williamson (in background with trumpet), Susan Cowsill
NASHVILLE, 1996

Listening to "Wasn't That a Mighty Storm"

Tom Rush
NASHVILLE, 1996

"Wasn't That a Mighty Storm"

Tom Rush, Emmylou Harris, Odetta, and Evie Kennedy
NASHVILLE, 1996

photos by Alan Messer

of my family came in through the port of Galveston. My mother's family came in from Aberdeen, in Scotland, through the port of Galveston. So when a second port of entry into the United States was totally wiped out by this hurricane, it was an amazingly significant historical event, though it's rarely celebrated as such. But that's where my blood flows. My ancestors came through the Gulf Stream from Scotland and Wales and in through the port of Galveston. So that, for me, is my Statue of Liberty. And it was wiped out by this storm. That's why this song has always meant so much.

Then you bring in all these people to sing it. Frank Christian, who arrived in Nashville that morning to work on this album, had just gotten a message that his father had died. His father, Frank, was a dear, dear man who had passed his love for music on to his son. Frank's parents had also been surrogate parents to me, fed me, taken care of me, so it was also a loss to me.

But when Frank called home, his mother said, "Frank, the wake is not until Saturday. Stay there. Do what your father would have wanted you to do. Work on this music. Then come home." So Frank took a verse. He sang, "And the flood it took my neighbor, took my brother, too. I thought I heard my father calling, and I watched my mother go," with regard to the storm sweeping across Galveston in 1900. Since everyone on this recording was family, in one sense or another, we knew what Frank was singing about, and it was overwhelming for all of us. It was hard to even get through the song. Tom Rush was playing it and saying, "I don't *believe* this."

John Hartford, who of course wrote "Gentle on My Mind" and provided the bass notes on "Wimoweh," is a cancer survivor but was not able to come in to the session because he was ill. His son, Jamie, who is a great writer and player himself, came in to fill in for his dad. He took the verse: "And trains they all were loaded,/The people were leaving town,/The trestle gave way to the water,/And the trains they went on down." And when he sings, you can hear his father singing. It's chill-inducing.

Then you had Odetta, who taught us all what soul is! When she comes in, you say, "Bless you." So it is extraordinary. And even the people on backing vocals, who range from Shawn Camp, a very young and wonderful songwriter in our own tradition, to Andrew Hardin, Tom Russell, Eric Taylor, and then to Doug Lancio, Ray Kennedy, Steve Earle, Tom Littlefield, and my dad. And there's Carolyn Hester, whose family also came in through the port of Galveston. My father and his sweetheart of twenty years, Yvonne Richards, both sang backup on "Mighty Storm." Yvonne sings with the Sweet Adelines, a women's barbershop quartet. On top of that, we had Emmylou Harris, Susan Cowsill, Lee Satterfield, Maura Kennedy, and Mary Ann Kennedy and Pam Rose, from the Kennedy-Rose Band. It's an extraordinary combination of voices.

Joe: *Why on earth didn't you consider ending the album with that song? It's a hell of a tough track to follow!*

Nanci: We did think of it. I suggested it to Rooney, but he said, "No, I think I know where this goes," and we talked about it quite a lot. We didn't want to end it on that note. "If I Had a Hammer" was meant to close this album.

Joe: *In much the same symbolic sense as Willie McTell's great line "Take this hammer . . ."?*

Nanci: And "give it to the captain." Exactly. As in passing this stuff on. So even though "Wasn't That a Mighty Storm" is so emotional and you can hear the emotion in everybody's voice, "If I Had a Hammer" was a greater representation of the generations and the genres of music all drawn together in one place, and of this process of passing on the music.

||: ___ s a m e   s o n g ,   s a m e   v o i c e ___ :||

A n o t h e r   p e r s p e c t i v e :
N a n c i   l i s t e n i n g   t o   p l a y b a c k

Isn't Jim Williamson's trumpet line good there? He's the same fella who played the flügelhorn on "Saint Teresa of Avila" [on *Blue Roses from the Moon*]. He's a wonderful horn player. And he was sitting on the floor during this recording because there were thirty-seven people around this cage of microphones, and he was so loud that we had to make him sit on the floor away from the microphone!

Listen to all those guitars! Doug Lancio, Tom Rush on slide bottleneck, and on banjo is Bela Fleck, and Bill Hearne is flat-pickin'. This song is so amazing because it was just sitting there in the Library of Congress, and Tom Rush and Eric Von Schmidt plucked it out of there. It is such a powerful narrative of a real event. *That* is folk music!

‖: s a m e   s o n g ,   a n o t h e r   v o i c e :‖

J I M   R O O N E Y

Tom Rush was one of the most popular artists in the folk revival of the sixties. He learned this song from Eric Von Schmidt and it turned out to be Tom's signature song. We were looking for something that would be a big group song. One of the definitive factors of that folk era was that there were certain songs that large groups of people could gather themselves around and throw their energy into. And . . . although this is a song about a terrible disaster, the tone almost is like dancing on the *Titanic,* celebrating the tragedy, or maybe marking what came out of that, what was learned.

But there is a problem when it comes to recording songs like this: when people are shouting, "Wasn't it sad when that ship went down?" they run the risk of not sounding sad at all! But in this case what I liked was the individual voices that gave voice to the actual tragedy in the song, like Jamie Hartford and Frank Christian. The way they delivered the line, especially Frank, because, yeah, as Nanci said to you, his father had died. And Frank could just as easily have gone home, but he stayed with us for a couple of days, and that told me something about the power of this music. Then he delivered that line in this song, with great feeling.

Although Tom Rush has done this song many, many times, this performance is the best I've heard. And I say that not just because I was in the room when it was being recorded. It has got a special power that comes from these different voices, where people are bringing their own lives and personalities to bear on it—sometimes, as with Frank Christian, bringing all that to bear on just a single line. That kind of stuff is what gives this lyric, this song, its emotional truth.

That is exactly what Nanci had in mind when she decided to do several of these large group songs, which, of course, are a recording engineer's nightmare. One reason I love to record with Nanci is that she likes to record live music as it is happening. Studios shouldn't be places where no live music is allowed. Fortunately, I'm working with Mark Miller, an engineer who is not scared of these things and actually welcomes them. And on this track in particular we were able to capture that very spontaneous element of recording that we prefer. And just as so many of the musicians Nanci works with are word-sensitive, that should also be a feature of a producer and an engineer. To me, the lyrics are the thing. The lyrics and the melody. I respect the word and the music, as written. That is the core of what we're working with. I want that material to be respected.

And so I'm not a big fan of players who don't listen. All the best players are great listeners. Just as all the great writers are listeners! Listening is one of the great arts. A lot of the time, people would be much better off if they were listening, especially musicians! And this is where Nanci's own group really came into their own.

Here they were, in one situation after another, presented with so many different styles of music, so many different people working around them. And I just can't say enough about them, as a group or as individuals, as far as their ability to give us a fundamental reading of a song that we can build on. That's not easy to come by. They really do travel into the center of a song without a lot of fuss.

And without a hell of a lot of direction, either. I think Nanci and I both get along because we like to let people find their way without being told what to do. I don't mind giving someone a couple of clues, but I really want it to come from them. That's because I really do believe we should help musicians find their own voices in this setting, not impose something on them from without. That's how you help musicians bring to the music that element of their own personalities which helps make a great voice, vocally and musically. That's why I will always choose to work with musicians whose personalities come through in the way they sing, beat a rhythm, play chords. And all of the people we worked with here have definite and individual characteristics. They are not clones, and they don't play generic music. In other words, they have their own voices, and that's what you hear on this album.

This group has been together for a while, and they've been with Nanci for a while, and the other players—Frank Christian, Andy Hardin, and the many other people who joined them—have had time together. So what comes across when you work with musicians of that caliber, in this context, is that nobody is trying to show off. They were paying full attention to the song and supporting the singers. That's a great gift. And it's also another element we all love in folk music. The musician doesn't show off at the expense of the song.

:|: **s a m e   s o n g ,   a n o t h e r   v o i c e** :|

D O U G   L A N C I O

You can barely hear me on this track, but what the hell, it was a fantastic session to work on. Just to be there when Odetta opened her mouth and you heard that sound! In terms of my electric guitar work here, the song has only two chords so there's barely any place to put anything, once you put that butter-knife guitar on. But once Odetta opens her mouth, near the end of the song you go, "Wow! I wish I had been playing more," because you just want to go [*imitates sound of guitar line sky-diving*]. It was stunning just to be there. And you're right to call this the Cecil B. DeMille track, because it really was just a matter of being present amid that cast of thousands. But what was great about this album was that on most other tracks everybody was free to play what they wanted, go where they felt they had to go, musically. During my whole gig on this album, the history of folk music was being taught to me just by being here.

:|: **s a m e   s o n g ,   a n o t h e r   v o i c e** :|

L E E   S A T T E R F I E L D ,   V O C A L S ,   M A N D O L I N

It was my idea to do the echo: "Wasn't that a mighty, wasn't that a mighty storm." And Nanci sent me in to lead the boys because they needed to be heavier, so she had me conduct the male orchestra. And it was really fun to do, believe me, even working out those harmonies. And it's powerful stuff, don't you think? Just to hear people sing out like that.

:|: **s a m e   s o n g ,   a n o t h e r   v o i c e** :|

P A M   R O S E ,   V O C A L S

There were so many people in there at the same time. That's something you don't often see in a session. It was incredible. Just to see Odetta, Emmylou,

*Nanci Griffith and Lee
Satterfield*
NASHVILLE, 1992

*photo from
Nanci Griffith's
personal collection*

*Jamie Hartford
"Wasn't That a Mighty
Storm"*
NASHVILLE, 1998

*photo by
Alan Messer*

*Jamie Hartford, Tom
Littlefield, Odetta
"Wasn't That a Mighty
Storm"*
NASHVILLE,
NOVEMBER 1996

*photo by
Alan Messer*

Carolyn Hester, Tom Rush, and be part of that with my Kennedy-Rose buddy, Mary Ann, was oozing magic.

And when you're singing out like that you feel emotional, tearful, transcendent, fired up by a sense of anticipation, when you have all these people singing these parts. When you're doing that live, you are on the edge, on an absolute high, musically. It's really pushing the envelope, living on the edge. And that sense comes across so often on this album, which to me is so gutsy, so organic, as everyone says.

To listen to an album where people are loving the joy and simplicity of playing together also reminds you what music should be all about. Likewise the idea of just getting there and singing, instead of spending two days EQ'ing the drum stool! That really was refreshing, great.

same song, another voice

TOM LITTLEFIELD

I was standing next to Odetta when she sang her solo part. As soon as she opened her mouth, my jaw dropped and the hair on the back of my neck stood straight up. While she was singing, I kept thinking, "How the hell does she do that?" What a beautiful memory!

deportee

Words and Music by Woody Guthrie and Martin Hoffman

Joe: *Woody Guthrie again, but this time a song about emigrants. Why this particular Guthrie composition?*

Nanci: This was a song Lucinda [Williams] and I would sing together late at night. "Deportee" captures that brilliant talent Woody had for reading the newspaper every morning from a journalist's point of view and then writing a song and telling the news that way. But though he did just tell the news, he also placed so much heart in it. He gave you a sense you were there.

It is like a campfire song that needs a lot of voices to tell this tale about Mexican farmworkers who had been shipped out of their country on a lousy plane that crashed in the desert, and nobody seemed to care. Woody put their story into the hearts of America and the world, so that these people would never be forgotten.

At first Rooney was saying, "We'll just do it with you and Lucinda, the way you used to sing it," but I said, "I've been talking to Steve Earle, and he's always wanted to sing a verse in that song."

I also said I'd like to include John Stewart because he is such a massive influence on me and is occasionally forgotten. He was a massive influence on lots of people, beginning with the Kingston Trio, then going off on his own and writing pop hits like "Daydream Believer" and "July, You're a Woman" and

left to right:
Lucinda
Williams,
Susan Cowsill,
Nanci Griffith,
John Stewart,
Odetta,
Peaches,
Steve Earle
NASHVILLE,
1996

"Deportee"
session
photo by
Alan Messer

211

Fleetwood Mac's "Gold." He certainly influenced me instrumentally. I borrow more things from John Stewart and Sonny Curtis than from anyone else, in terms of the way I play guitar, the voicings, and so on. I'm not a complicated guitar player, but I think I'm very good at playing Nanci Griffith. Whereas Sonny Curtis would say I'm very good at playing Sonny Curtis and that if you ask me to do something else I'm no damn good!

John Stewart would tell you the same thing. John and I did that duet of his song "Sweet Dreams Will Come" on my *Little Love Affairs* album. . . . We were playing the Queen Victoria Theatre in London, and he was going to sit in with us. So I stayed up all night learning the song in standard tuning so I could play it and say, "Hey, John, look what I can do." And he came in and said, "Nanci, I play that in a drop D, and you play things in that tuning all the time! Why didn't you figure that out? You only have to move your fingers two or three times in that tuning, whereas if you play it in a standard tuning you're all over the board!" I was so embarrassed.

Joe: *For this track you also brought in your replacement, once removed, from those days you spent with Bill and Bonnie Hearne.*

Nanci: Yeah, Tish Hinojosa, who sang in Spanish, which seems quite perfect for this song. And even though it is a cast of thousands you hear singing, solo voices still sound out above all that. It is, to me, an extraordinary recording.

Joe: *It's also political.*

Nanci: That's another reason I wanted to record it. America prides itself on being a melting pot for all races, a place for all people to come, from around the world. So the song, which is a true story, has always meant a lot to me, in that we've gone through times in our history in America where that hasn't been particularly true.

⟦: same song, same voice :⟧

Another perspective:
Nanci listening to playback

[*Responding to opening lines*] "Lucinda and I sound like Sarah and Maybelle [Carter]. I think Woody would have liked that, and the combination of Tish's voice, singing those lines in Spanish. It was my idea to have Tish do the Spanish part because I thought it was something that had always been missing: the [Spanish] language itself. Before this, it was, like, sing about these people, but don't use their own language. Spanish needed to be there. And that's Fats Kaplin on the accordion, which lent the recording such a Mexican campfire flavor.

See what I mean about Odetta's voice and how authoritative it sounds? [*Responding to Odetta's line, "Is this the best way we can grow our big orchards?"*] Like the voice of God! Maybe she should be up there on Mount Rushmore next to Washington, Jefferson, Teddy Roosevelt, or next to Crazy Horse, a hundred miles away from those lads.

Peaches, my dog, was there in the studio and would stay at my feet all the time, but she would perk up when it was Odetta's turn to sing, and go and lie down under the B-3 organ! And when Odetta stepped away from the mike, Peaches would come back. It was like Odetta willed the dog to move away for a while, without even saying anything. It was great fun to watch. And that is how powerful a presence Odetta is—even dogs step back when she sings!

⟦: same song, another voice :⟧

JIM ROONEY

What strikes me about this song is that it is still so true, even though it was written—what, fifty years ago? It could have been written today. It really makes you mad. And Odetta really came through in this song in such a commanding way. Her delivery of that lyric, "Is this the best that we can do?" sums up the emotion in the song: anger, outrage at the idea that these social injustices continue and that we allow them to go on so that we can have a peach on our table, or whatever. It's not just about Mexicans being exploited, or any individual race; it's people around the world. You could extend this song to include people who wear Nike shoes, as a criticism of our system of labor, where the world allows such things to happen. Woody's song says all that, though the original circumstances related to a specific incident where a plane crashed, which was carrying migrant workers. It applies to everywhere and everyone.

So when people say to me, "Hasn't that song been done a lot? Hasn't it been done enough?" I say, "Evidently not." I'm all for doing it again. And I think the performances of the different people in this song, and the different voices, especially Odetta's voice, just make the message of this song inescapable.

As a producer, there is the challenge of approaching a song that has been done so often. That, too, on this album, was the challenge of "Hard Times" and "Mighty Storm." Many of these songs have been done often, and I'm sure some people will say, "Give them a rest."

I've been singing some songs for almost fifty years, and there are certain songs I just don't get tired of singing. And one thing common to so many of the songs I still love singing is that they have a lot of emotion in them, a lot of energy in there. And that energy is not going to go away. The challenge is to get at that energy. And the idea Nanci had for this record, in terms of bringing all these voices around these songs, was to try to get back in touch with that energy. Nanci chose people who have a great commitment to music, to their own art, to these songs. When all those energies collide, you really do get something special. And I think that is what happens here on "Deportee," which has its own innate energy and integrity. All of that comes across here, and that is what really makes great music. And it really is easier to make a song breathe again, if it's true, as is the case with so much of what Woody Guthrie wrote.

‖: s a m e   s o n g ,   a n o t h e r   v o i c e :‖

LUCINDA WILLIAMS

The whole idea of folk music is that you are telling a story behind something that actually happened, interpreting it, just like Woody Guthrie did in

"Deportee." As a singer you have to stay true to that. Singing this song, you just remember that although Woody was in the thick of a particular political situation back then, this stuff about deportees is still happening in America today. He was sympathetic, empathetic, with the plight of these people, so it's easy to tune in to at that level. Singing a song like this keeps you close to what the songs are about, close to political realities.

And when I sing this song, I realize we are carrying on the tradition, which is like going back to where I came from. I started out doing this kind of song. Those are the roots of my own music. I started out doing traditional stuff, then moved into contemporary folk, like Dylan, but I started out with the John and Alan Lomax *Folk Song U.S.A.* books that Nanci probably still has too. So I identify with songs like "Deportee" at that level. It all feels real natural to me. After all, the first album I did, in 1978, was on Folkways, and it was all other people's songs. I think Nanci has just taken that idea one step further, inviting a lot of her friends and people she admires to join in with her in this. It's a great idea. It's like that [*Lucinda nods her head in the direction of the sing-along that is going on in the next room, where about a dozen voices are singing "Deportee"*]. That's how we all started out, sitting around, singing these songs with people we know. She's just taken that and put it on a record. And so the circle continues.

photo by Alan Messer

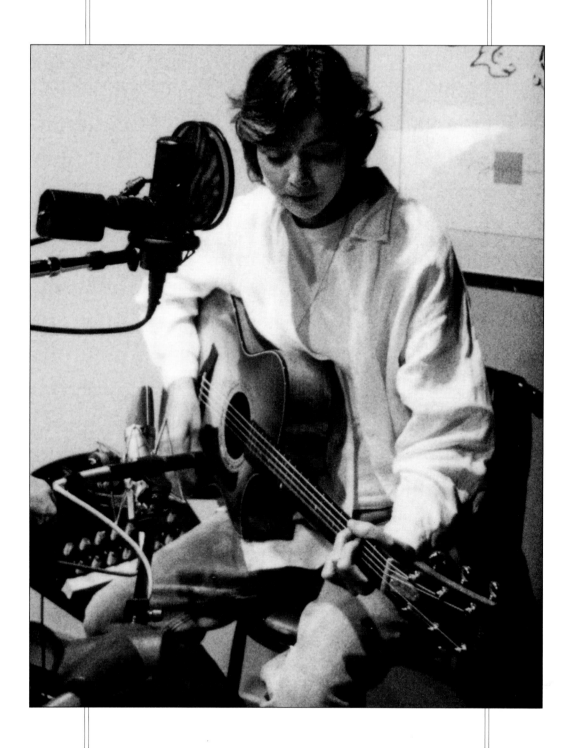

19

yarrington
town

Words and Music by Mickie Merkins

Joe: *This is another relatively contemporary song.*

Nanci: Yeah, it was written by Mickie Merkins, a dear friend of mine from Austin who is such an incredibly talented writer that people keep going back to her for songs. I know I did. I've been listening to this song for fifteen years now and have always loved it because it's about a woman's coming-of-age. But it's also the essence of what you and I talked about earlier—that people must finally become their own home, form their own center. Emmy loves this song, Carolyn loves this song, and we all wanted to pass it on to the next generation.

It definitely was important for Emmylou and Carolyn to sing this song to their daughters. Their daughters are all singers, players. And the song basically tells them, and reminds so many of us, that you can't project an image onto a man and make him the center of the rest of your life, that you have to be a person within yourself.

Joe: *It sure is a healthy lesson to learn, for either sex.*

Nanci: It is. I know many men who still haven't learned that lesson, who project everything of who they are onto a woman

Nanci Griffith
August
1997

Other Voices,
Other Rooms
*photo by
Alan Messer*

217

and expect her to sustain that—in other words, they have no identity of their own. But women, especially, have to learn that lesson too, because it's something you're not taught. In fact, you are taught to go out and find that person who will become the center of your life. Originally we had planned on recording the first verse, where the mothers tell the daughters not to do that, then let the daughters take over from there. They did a beautiful job, but when Jim and I mixed it, we finally decided that although Carolyn and Emmylou were saying something to their daughters and the daughters sang it beautifully when they took over, nothing could beat these two mothers. So we pulled the daughters into the backing vocals and ended up using Carolyn and Emmy's original scratch vocals—the voices you set down when you are recording the song, if the people aren't there who will do the final version.

Joe: *At any point during that session did you wish you had a daughter here that you could sing to?*

Nanci: No. It was like "Turn Around" from the first *Other Voices* album; I felt all the images. James Hooker, who has two daughters, was totally in tears; so was Chet Atkins. But while I can relate to the feeling that one's children are growing up and will soon be gone, that doesn't make me want to have a child of my own.

same song, same voice

Another perspective:
Nanci listening to playback

Here come the mothers now [*responding to the line, "And the time it flies quickly"*]. Here I'm listening to all the music, all the players, because they played so beautifully on this song. And as I was trying to say earlier, some writers write so much in character that you end up with their phrasing when you're singing a song.

Even though Mickie Merkins isn't a singer, you can't sing her songs without *her* phrasing coming out of your mouth. [*Responding to the line, "And he promised to love me as long as I'd*

Meghan Ahern and mother, Emmylou Harris; Nanci Griffith; Carolyn Hester and
daughter, Amy Blum

NASHVILLE, 1996

photo by Alan Messer

stay"] That just brings tears to my eyes because you can hear these two women telling their daughters, "Don't make these mistakes." It's a wonderful piece of writing. Wonderful. And Carolyn and Emmy are just so beautiful together.

╠ same song, another voice ╣

JIM ROONEY

I love this song and this performance because it sounds like an old song, it has the feeling of an old song, and maybe it is an old song! Like Nanci, many people feel that they are tuning in to some other time, some other place, when they are writing a song. I have never talked to Mickie about this song, but that's my impression, that it *is* an old song.

╠ same song, another voice ╣

CAROLYN HESTER

No matter what Nanci says about Jim Rooney getting mixed up about the sound of our voices—and it is so sweet of her to say that—I feel the three voices on "Yarrington Town" are really distinctive because of the different ranges. I had to sing the fifth because I've got that higher range.

I love this recording. Nanci is so professional that it was a wonder to watch the whole thing evolve. And it seems to me that everything that has happened in her life has come into play for these recordings. From her early love of Buddy Holly and the Crickets, through to starting out touring with me, getting her own band on the road, and now going back to base, back to her father's love of folk music, her family upbringing. It's all here.

Of course this album is a history of folk music, but it's also a personal history of Nanci Griffith, to the soul. And she really did work hard on this. She's one of the most dedicated workers I have ever seen. And I feel that great success couldn't happen to a better, nicer, or more capable person, especially in terms of these two folk albums, which bring her and so many of us back to our folk roots. I'm really proud to be part of the whole project, from the gig in Carnegie Hall to the time we shot the video in Austin and right up to this recording of "Yarrington Town." It's been a blessing to me.

These albums contain some phenomenal work. I've no problem saying that. And I don't know anyone who could have done this as well as Nanci, from the original idea for the first album right up to the whole concept of this second album and the book. I think it will take most people a long time to realize the work, the dreams, the labor of love that went into all this. And I hear all that when I listen to "Yarrington Town."

‖: s a m e   s o n g ,   a n o t h e r   v o i c e :‖

Emmylou Harris

Recording these albums was like being at a family reunion: lots of folks you hadn't seen in a long time, some you'd never met but had heard stories about. I even got to sing for the first time with one of my own daughters, and I'll always be grateful to Nanci for the vision which inspired that event.

[Recording] "Yarrington Town" is a sweet memory for me, made even sweeter by its being part of this extraordinary musical quilt that Nanci has lovingly pieced together with her delicate but very capable hands.

i still
miss someone

Words and Music by Roy Cash Jr.

Joe: *You say that although this was one of Johnny Cash's earliest hits, he never claimed he composed it.*

Nanci: No, he always said it was written by his brother Roy. I chose this above many other Johnny Cash songs simply because I've always loved it. As a young girl, in every backup role I played, I had to sing the harmony to this. It was always part of the repertoire, always that popular. And to have Rodney Crowell—which gave us a John Cash connection, because he, of course, was married to Roseanne Cash—and to have the Crickets made it even more special. Initially, I was going to play guitar on this, but Sonny Curtis gave it such a strong flavor of his own that I backed out of playing with Rodney. Sonny just picked up his guitar and played this extraordinary augmented thing that has so much character and is so beautiful that I just put my guitar down.

Joe: *You put your guitar down quite a lot during the recording of this album.*

Nanci Griffith
1993

photo by
David Gahr

Nanci: I did! We had so many brilliant players, and if my guitar voicing was on there, it would have wiped out their voicing. So it was more important for me to capture their voicing.

223

Joe: *Other voices?*

Nanci: Exactly, in every sense! Though I did play rhythm on "Who Knows Where the Time Goes" and on "Streets of Baltimore" and maybe two others.

Joe: *How do you rate John Cash as an American folk artist?*

Nanci: He's a genre all his own, like Richard Thompson. There is no space to put Johnny Cash, because he's had pop hits, country hits, folk hits, and now folk grunge! I especially like his latest albums because they are just straight-on Johnny Cash, and that, to me, is pure folk music from the 1990s.

same song, same voice

Another perspective:
Nanci listening to playback

This just feels so good. But John does this so much faster, almost in a 4/4 time, whereas I always thought of it as a ballad. But it felt right to us to do it at that pace. Simple and beautiful.

same song, another voice

JIM ROONEY

This is one of those country songs I've known and done for a long, long time. And we wanted to have something country in this collection. Country *was* folk music, at one time. Most of it's not now, though I'd definitely agree with Nanci when she says that the purest form of country-folk is being carried on by people like Iris DeMent and Gillian Welch. Absolutely. And Johnny Cash is *the* true folk artist, more than any of us.

Something about "I Still Miss Someone" is so perfect, in terms of its mood and its simplicity, which I've always liked. And I think Nanci wanted that quality to be represented here. It's a side of Johnny Cash that maybe isn't so well known. It's the lyrical side and also the person who is very quiet and reflective underneath it all. That's the mood about this song that I love. The understatement of it is very telling: "I still miss someone." You couldn't get more understated than that, when you're basically saying, "My heart is crushed."

And we achieved that understatement with the Crickets. I think they give it a feel that is very true to the song. As does Rodney's singing of it. But of course he was involved with the Cash family for a long time, and he had a certain emotional reality about this song that draws on that experience of being married to Roseanne Cash. So, in a way, this recording reflects some of Johnny Cash's influence on all of us.

same song, another voice

RODNEY CROWELL, SINGER-SONGWRITER

I had lots of reasons for playing on this song. One was that it was written by my former father-in-law's brother. I'd sung this song all my life. I'd sit at home on the side of the bed and sing it. And I'd sing it live with my band. It's such a poetic song. "At my door the leaves are falling. A cold wild wind . . ."—it's almost like those cowboy ballads that are made up of really simple poetry.

It's also a great sentiment about lost love, like "You Are My Sunshine," that kind of big song, on a simple line. It also sings well. I wish I had written it. And this version sounded good to me. I sounded kinda pinched and nasal, and Nanci sounded fine and free. That's a pretty cool mix.

same song, another voice

J. I. ALLISON

Playing on this really was like a back-to-base thing for me because it's a country swing deal, which is what I started playing when I was just thirteen, in Lubbock, Texas. That's when I was with country bands, playing Hank Thompson songs, all that. So being on this particular session really felt like coming back home.

try
the love

Words and Music by Pat McLaughlin

Joe: *Pat McLaughlin?*

Nanci: I've known Pat since I used to go to the Northeast in 1981 into that folk scene. Then we met after he moved to Nashville around the same time I started recording here, 1983. And I've been a massive fan ever since.

Joe: *Why? Because he moves so much when he sings, as you say, onstage?*

Nanci: Yes. He has the most moving body parts of any person I have ever seen—and that includes Elvis! Pat is an incredible writer, and like me, he's written many hits for other people. His music is like a blend of New Orleans blues and bluegrass. No one else would ever put those two together. He's as comfortable being a wonderful rhythm guitar player for Jamie Hartford as he is playing mandolin with John Prine or as he is standing with Nanci Griffith and the Blue Moon Orchestra singing his song "Try the Love." He wrote me a lovely letter telling me what it means to him to be included in this project. He is a brilliant man, full of soul.

"Try the Love" is such a great song. We've all felt the way this song describes. You know this person isn't going to take

Nanci Griffith
1997

photo by
Señor
McGuire

227

this up—reciprocate your feelings. It's a wish for something you can't have, it's just "I've got a home here; I can't unpack." It's an incredibly well written song. When I first heard the song I couldn't understand what Pat was saying, but it's "Try the love that the keeper of the keys told me one time was clearly not for me. He's not keeping no more." Since he had mentioned the keys, I thought he said, "He's not keeping the door"!

The session was wonderful. James and I spent about a half hour writing the overture for "Try the Love." Then we started the song, and Pat was jump-started because he's got to come in. And we sang it from top to bottom, not a word missed, not a phrasing wrong, got it on just the second take.

|: s a m e   s o n g ,   s a m e   v o i c e :|

A n o t h e r   p e r s p e c t i v e ;
N a n c i   l i s t e n i n g   t o   p l a y b a c k

[*Responding to orchestral introduction*] Here, I'm listening to that beautiful guitar part that sounds like a seagull, that Philip Donnelly does during our concerts, though Doug plays it here. And I just love the humor of this song. It's such a sweet song of longing! But the humor in the lyrics is so typically Pat McLaughlin. Bad things happen for a reason, and good things come out of bad things—that type of attitude. And Pat McInerney is just so subtle a percussionist.

|: s a m e   s o n g ,   a n o t h e r   v o i c e :|

JIM ROONEY

Pat McLaughlin has always been one of the great things about the Nashville music scene. Pat has been playing ever since I came here twenty years ago. He's never become a big star, but his music is extremely compelling, as far as I'm concerned. I've done a couple of albums with him, and he really has a very rootsy thing about his music. It's very grounded, rooted. Pat's music implies roots going into the ground, into the dirt.

The whole thing has an integrity that seems to work so well in the song. And I like the idea of Nanci using an orchestral prelude to "Try the Love."

After all, way back, the Weavers were using orchestral backings, though a lot of people didn't like that at the time and still don't. "Ain't No Mountain High Enough" uses a sixty-second orchestral overture, and that's Motown. But I took no vow of purity! James Hooker and Nanci cooked up that prelude, and I think it works great, as both a prelude and a form of interlude.

⫸ same song, another voice ⫷
PAT McLAUGHLIN

photo by Greg Gorman

I was pleasantly surprised when Nanci chose this song, then asked me to sing on it. It's a song I wrote about fifteen years ago, on the front porch of a house I used to live in, and I wasn't trying to write a waltz. It just became that kind of song. It was a gut-wrencher for me at the time—one of those involuntary songs. But it is also one of those songs that take the pain out of songwriting, because they do come quite naturally. And too rarely! It also was written early in my career, like those songs you write before you learn too much about songwriting. Maybe that helped, too. It comes from some instinctive, emotional level.

Pat McLaughlin

The session was pretty unusual; we weren't going to do the song too many times, and that was a nice feeling, though I wish I'd been in a little better voice that day.

⫸ same song, another voice ⫷
DOUG LANCIO

Working with Nanci has been a real education in folk music. I come from a rock background, so I've been discovering all this stuff while I'm with her. And one thing I noticed is that there is really not that much difference, musically, between rock and folk. It's just a matter of a decibel or so. I've simply had to learn to play more quietly.

22

streets
of baltimore

Words and Music by Harlan Howard and Tom-Paul Glaser

Joe: *This song is your tribute to your mentor, Harlan Howard.*

Nanci: Definitely. And it is typical Harlan Howard. I've recorded Harlan Howard songs over the years, like "Never Mind," which was used in the movie *The Firm*. Nobody else could ever take two farmworkers and make their story the lost love letter of the century, which "Never Mind" is!

For people who don't know who Harlan Howard is, he's not just a country songwriter. He was the father of the Bakersfield sound, which, to me, is the beginning of country rock and roll and which makes him such a big hero of people like Dwight Yoakam.

Harlan wrote "Tiger by the Tail" and "Pick Me Up on Your Way Down" and "Heartaches by the Numbers" for Buck Owens, and they all have that upright doo-wop bass, which is the beginning of that whole sound. And you had Conway Twitty and people like that, who, although they were rock and roll, took the sound in a totally different direction than, say, the guys in Memphis. When you hear Harlan do "I Fall to Pieces," which he wrote for Patsy Cline, it's got that same bass run to it, that same syncopation. He also wrote a lot of Patsy Cline's other hits.

"Streets of Baltimore," to me, has always been the definitive

Nanci Griffith
1997

photo by
Señor
McGuire

231

Harlan Howard song. Basically because, Harlan being my mentor, I know his history. He was an orphan, raised in foster homes, went into the military, and while he was training he was given a message that there was another Howard on the base. Harlan met him, and it was his brother, Milton, whom he mentions in "Never Mind." But "Streets of Baltimore" had this sadness that Harlan carried. You can hear the sadness in this fella's heart. He was virtually abandoned from early childhood. And the only good thing about it is his wife, Melanie, who has gone back and found out that the social workers kept more notes on Harlan's history than would a parent! There are more notes on what Harlan Howard was like in those years than there would be on any other child. Like the fact that he was sent to work in a farming community when he was twelve, but he had fallen in love with this social worker and convinced himself that she was in love with him as well. Then he gets out to this farm, gets up early, works every day, and doesn't like it, so he runs away.

They found him sitting on the stoop of the social worker's house in Ann Arbor, and they said, "What are you doing here? Did they hit you? Hurt you?"

And his reply, at twelve, was, "No, it's just I can't see myself shoveling manure all my life."

He had more to do in his life, thank God, than shovel manure! And this song, "Streets of Baltimore," has echoes of all that history.

Five years later, at seventeen, he was writing songs like "Call Me Mr. In-Between," which was recorded by Burl Ives and by Mel Tormé. But talk about missing verses! I heard a demo of Harlan doing it, which Ray Stevens had produced back before he himself became a singer, and it contains a verse that was missing from both [of the other] versions. I certainly don't remember hearing this verse as a child. Had I heard it, I certainly would have remembered it. Any child would. It goes, "All of the men walk around with their babies, driving in their cars, with their arms round the ladies, while I walk around like a dog with the rabies. They just call me Mr. In-Between." Ain't that something? Had I heard that from Burl Ives when I was a child, boy, that would have been something special, wouldn't it?

Joe: *So Harlan was also the first punk-country songwriter!*

Nanci: He sure was! He was a rebel of his time whose lyrics were of honest clarity and true to his social era. He wrote "Busted," which was a hit for Ray Charles and so many others. He's had sixty number one songs and over nine hundred covers of his songs! He's the only songwriter in the United States National Songwriters Hall of Fame who ever wrote a country song. The rest of them are the Ira Gershwins and Cole Porters, but no country songwriters.

Joe: *Do you think, then, that institutions like the Songwriters Hall of Fame should be broken down and started all over again?*

Nanci: Most big institutions like that do need to be broken down, yes. That's part of what folk music is all about right now, for me, taking things back to the basics, starting again, giving credit where credit is long overdue. That's part of the impulse behind these two albums.

Joe: *Most rock institutions, such as the Rock and Roll Hall of Fame, are, as you suggest, sexist, or maybe more specifically they want to celebrate the kind of masculine values embodied in the choice of rockers they recognize. Everything else seems to be undervalued.*

Nanci: I think that is true. And it's pretty much something that only a few women have managed to overcome. Bonnie Raitt is one; she's held in respect by every musician. But a lot of times you do get written off if you are a woman. You do have to write songs that are twice as good, play guitar twice as well as a rock guy, in order to get the same amount of attention. You do seem to be more accepted if you want to be idolized for your appearance.

Joe: *You moved against stereotypes in the music industry, particularly in terms of country-folk, at the beginning of your career, when you funded your first four albums and retained controlling interest and economic independence.*

Nanci: I did finance my first four albums, went to the bank, said, "I would like to do this. Will you give me a loan?" And they did! Each album was a separate project, and so, yes, I do retain the rights to those albums, which have, of course, more than paid their way.

Joe: *What was the response when you delivered to a record company albums* *you had financed, written, helped to produce, and intended to retain publishing rights on?*

Nanci: Shock. Because in the music industry it was somewhat unheard of at that time. It's being done all the time now, with artists producing their own albums and leasing them to the label, but back in 1977 it was something new.

Joe: *But the position of a woman—in country music, in particular—is, historically, decorative. Either that or you have women like Patsy Cline and Brenda Lee, who arrive in the studio owned by, say, the Bradleys, who then record the voice and send the singer home, leaving the shaping and selling of the product to the producers—and leaving the bulk of the profits in their hands rather than the hands of the artists.*

Nanci: That is very true, just as it is in the rock world. I'm sure it's true even for acts like the Spice Girls. But things did begin to change in country music when K. T. Oslin came along. She was enormously talented in terms of doing her own work. But Nashville is definitely very "girl singer" oriented. They don't want you tampering with writing or producing. It's like "Leave that to the boys." But things change. One of Harlan Howard's favorite songwriters is Cindy Walker, who has never left West Texas. She wrote Orbison hits like "Sweet Dreams, Baby," and "You Don't Know Me" for Ray Charles, as well as hits for Dean Martin, Bing Crosby, and many more.

Joe: *But if you move too far against the Nashville establishment, as, say, k. d. lang did, you do tend to get ostracized.*

Nanci: Yes. But then I've always been ostracized. I've never been part of the Nashville establishment. I was let in only because great singers like Kathy Mattea, Jan Brown, Suzy Boguss, Maura O'Connell, Willie Nelson, and Emmylou Harris have recorded my songs and had hits with them. Therefore they let me have a table in the corner, occasionally, at the CMA gathering.

Nashville is an industry city above everything else, and if you are making money for them, you are in. If you're not, you're out. And that applies whether you are a woman or a man, though a lot of the time, if you're doing well on MTV or VH-1 no one in Nashville knows about it, because they only know what's going on in the country music charts.

John Prine
1 9 9 3

photo from
Nanci Griffith's
personal collection

Harlan Howard, Nanci
Griffith, Darius Rucker, Jim
"Soni" Sonefeld
NASHVILLE, 1997

Harlan is the writer of hun-
dreds of hit songs, including
"Streets of Baltimore" on
Other Voices, Too

photo by
Alan Messer

John Prine, Nanci Griffith,
Harlan Howard, and
Burt Stein at the recording
session for "Streets of
Baltimore"
AUGUST 1997

Harlan Howard
NASHVILLE, 1997

Harlan Howard
NASHVILLE, 1997

photos by Alan Messer

Joe: *To get back to giving credit where credit is due, let's give credit to Tom-Paul Glaser, the co-writer of "Streets of Baltimore."*

Nanci: Of the Glaser Brothers. Well, they are adored in country music, and Tommy wrote a couple of other hits for Bobby Bare and the like. But the Glaser Brothers have been very instrumental in keeping country music in the center.

Joe: *And the session for "Streets of Baltimore"?*

Nanci: It was special because Harlan sat in the studio watching, waiting for his narrative to come around.

:| same song, same voice |:

Another perspective:
Nanci listening to playback

I loved doing this song as close as possible to the Bobby Bare production as we could, even in terms of the strings we put on. Ray Stevens had done the string arrangement for Bobby Bare's version, so we just used the same string arrangement. It's so 1950s. [*Responding to Harlan Howard's narration*] Doesn't his voice sound so resonant, so rich? And there is so much history there.

Harlan will bring out a word or a turn of phrase that has not been used in a poetic sense in modern music. It is a technique he uses to keep his art fresh. When he and I wrote "Say It Isn't So" for my *Flyer* album, Harlan wrote down the word "indicate" on the lyric page and, in the end, developed the line "Indicate that you're already reaching for the door." He said it was his melodic word for the day. It's a brilliant writing exercise and an unusual one for songwriters. A lot of writers could learn from that.

Nanci Griffith, Harlan Howard, and John Prine

AUGUST 1997

photo by Alan Messer

same song, another voice

JIM ROONEY

We definitely wanted to do a Harlan Howard song. This wasn't a duet or a boy-girl song, but Nanci figured out a way to make it work in that sense, so she does it with John Prine. And as a country song, "Streets of Baltimore," like "I Still Miss Someone" and "Wings of a Dove," finds its way onto the folk side of the street. Bobby Bare did a lot of that type of material—"500

nanci griffith's other voices

238

Miles" and so on. Those were basically story songs, as is "The Streets of Baltimore." It really is a crystallization of the lives of people who came from the farm to the city, then went back to the farm, and Harlan captures all that in two verses! And he is a master of that form of songwriting. And that's why the song wound up on this collection.

We wanted to have Harlan on this record, frankly, because he has been a great influence on us and on Nashville. And he has been extremely support- ive of Nanci. He sought Nanci out when he heard "Love at the Five-and- Dime," and he wanted to become her friend and be with her, as a writer, which tells you something about Harlan Howard! He is a writer first and foremost; that's all he thinks about. And he wants to be around other writers because he thinks that makes him better. He is a much admired veteran songwriter who still strives to write the best song of his life.

23

darcy
farrow

Words and Music by Tom Campbell and Steve Gillette

Joe: *Back to the sadness that links a lot of these songs.*

Nanci: Yes, and it was written by Tom Campbell and Steve Gillette, and both have written wonderful stuff. Tom Campbell worked for a long number of years with Jackson Browne. He now works for Gloria Steinem and heads up her Avocado Productions, raising money for Voters for Choice and battered women's shelters.

He and Steve were in college in the early sixties, close to Reno, Nevada, and had a folklore class. They were supposed to find a piece of folklore about that area, but they were too busy being boys and having fun. So they sat down the night before and wrote "Darcy Farrow" and handed it in as their folklore project, and of course it's totally fiction! They got an A because all their professors believed this story was true! It's a beautiful piece of writing.

John Denver had a hit with "Darcy Farrow." Every bluegrass band does this tune, but they always made a big production of it. I was working with Tom at a Voters for Choice concert, and I said, "Tom, will you sit down and write out the original lyrics? I want to strip the song down and sing it a cappella." Just like the Stephen Foster song, I wanted to bring it back to the writer's original vision. Tom typed it out on the

Nanci Griffith and Peaches
LOS
ANGELES,
1997

Playback
photo by
Alan Messer

241

computer, and we went to the studio and recorded it with just Pat McInerney's conga drums and my voice. Pat is such a remarkable musician. "Darcy Farrow" wouldn't breathe without his congas. And it is so stark—as stark as that part of Nevada. It is so stark, you can see the Truckee River, see the story of this girl and these two lovers. This is another one of these hidden little jewels on this record.

When it was all finished I sent it off to Steve Gillette, who is still writing songs, and he adored the fact that it was stripped down. But he raised the question of a missing verse! He said, "My verse got left out!" And I dug through everything I owned, and sure enough, I found the physical description that Steve had written: "Her voice was as sweet as sugar candy"—that's the verse I left out or, rather, Tom left out. So if anybody wants to blame someone for that missing verse, it is not my fault. Tom Campbell did it!

Joe: *You talk of stripping songs down. What do you think of Springsteen's moves in this direction,* The Ghost of Tom Joad?

Nanci: I went to the opening night of the concerts, and I was very moved by the things that were written from his own sense of place. And by what he had taken from Steinbeck. I'm a huge Bruce Springsteen fan and always have been. There's never been a preshow or interlude show tape of mine that didn't include Bruce Springsteen. But even so, watching him do *Tom Joad* I was aware he was writing a piece of fiction, instead of writing from his own sense of place. In his other work you always get the sense that the characters who fill his songs are not just people he knew from New Jersey but that if you went there you would see them on the streets, and you would know them. I really would like to see more artists strip their music back, though, like Springsteen did in *Joad*—if they want to.

I remember the last time I went out on tour, with just John Prine, and I had terrible stage fright because I had not been out without the Blue Moon Orchestra for so long. John had to console me every night, push me out there, so I know it's not easy to just stand there with a guitar, as Springsteen did.

Joe: *What do you think of the whole "unplugged" phenomenon, which often reveals the folk roots of rock and roll?*

Nanci: It does, and that's why, to me, the best "unplugged" album was

Tom Campbell
SANTA FE,
NEW MEXICO, 1973

photo by Jack Parson

Nirvana. I was a big Nirvana fan to begin with, but that gave me a greater understanding of the band and of Kurt [Cobain] and the music. And to see him with an acoustic guitar was really revealing. The most striking track was "About a Girl." Listening to that I got the sense that this was it. This was why I was a fan. So many people had said, "How can you be a fan of this grunge rock and roll?" And I'd say, "Call it grunge if you want, but they've taken all this stuff and come up with something that is very fresh and identifiably their own." And at some intrinsic level it is folk music.

Joe: *We've talked a lot about older voices. Who, among contemporary performers, moves you in the same way as, say, Carolyn Hester does?*

Nanci: There's this young artist, Matthew Ryan, who co-wrote "Everything's Comin' Up Roses" with me, and he's only twenty-five. When I first heard Matthew, I said, "This kid is really special." And for me it's still the voice of punk rock and folk punk. Jay Joyce, Tom Littlefield—still brilliant voices. Glen Phillips, Toad the Wet Sprocket. Adam Duritz and Counting Crows and Hootie and the Blowfish.

Joe: *Though one is loath to lump performers together simply in terms of gender, how do you rate the latest group of female singer-songwriters, like Alanis Morissette and Joan Osborne?*

Nanci: I like Alanis Morissette, and I especially like Joan Osborne, because she's got that blues base. She takes things back to a very good place in my childhood that was occupied by Janis Joplin. It is the blues base and a very selfless base and an ideological base that comes from the heart and says, "No, I'm not going to wear that. I'll dress as I please. I'm not going to be your Barbie doll." I always hated Barbie dolls. And going back to someone like Joni Mitchell, I'll always stand in line to buy the next Joni album.

𝄆 s a m e s o n g , a n o t h e r v o i c e 𝄇

JIM ROONEY

After all the other voices in this album I felt it was very important to just get back to Nanci's voice. And in the song department, to get a song down to the bones, to remind people that this is the way it starts. A voice, a song, and an instrument—or even no instrument. "Darcy Farrow" is another song that a lot of people believe is an old ballad, though it's relatively new.

The first album was focused more on bringing people's attention to the other writers who had influenced her and whose work she admired. In this album we were still doing that, but the focus was more on these *other voices* that have influenced her. And I think it is really good that Nanci is using the leverage she has to educate her audience, to tell them that there are other people they should check out. I can't say enough about that. Merle Haggard, at the height of his career, did a tribute to Jimmie Rodgers and a tribute to Bob Wills. Those albums probably didn't sell that well, but he felt it was important to tell people that they needed to pay attention to this stuff and not forget it. Nanci feels that way about Dave Van Ronk and Odetta and Carolyn Hester, all these different people we invited to be part of this record. She wants people to become aware and expand their horizons, and that is a really good and important thing to do.

𝄆 s a m e s o n g , a n o t h e r v o i c e 𝄇

PAT MCINERNEY

Nanci said, "I want to do this simply, basically with just the voice, but I want you to do something with me." She doesn't know the ins and outs of what the drums are. She just knows they are over there, and because we've worked together so long she knows she can trust me, knows I always approach stuff in terms of the lyric. I always have a lyric sheet before I do anything, and she likes that aspect in what we do.

The whole story of Darcy has this feel of somebody on horseback, to me. And when it says, "The river runs down to the Carson Valley plain," I see that as a horse and rider. And part of the lyric is that the girl falls from her horse and is killed. So I wanted that clip-clop sound. I got it by keeping the conga very damp, as in thick and solid, not at all Latin. And I tried to give the feeling that, as the story unfolds, you are on a journey. I went for the hypnotic potential in rhythms, as in the way I play that triplet and it doesn't have to move up. That kind of rhythm does draw you into a trance-like state, and that's exactly the mood and feeling I wanted so much to create in "Darcy Farrow."

Pat McInerney,
drummer/percussionist
1 9 9 6

photo by
Alan Messer

if i had
a hammer

Words and Music by Pete Seeger

Joe: *Let's talk about the song that you chose to close the album, "If I Had a Hammer." Tell me more about your vision of this track as an extension of that line, "Take this hammer, take it to the captain."*

Nanci: We close the album with this because it brought me full circle back to my childhood, with my father playing the Weavers. So, to me, it is exactly the same as singing, "Take this hammer, take it to the captain" and tell him I'm gone. It's like, "I'm out of here now, I've done my gig, but pass it on."

Joe: *In Leonard Cohen's songs "the captain" is usually God. Is it the same for you?*

Nanci: No. In songs like this "the captain" is just the man, the boss, whoever's got the big stick, not God. So it's like "Tell him I'm out of here. I don't need your cast-iron shackles."

Joe: *Like what? Maybe "Get me those two angels, Griffith and Prine, and let me fly right out of here, boss"? Or fly as you did as a kid when you heard the voice of Carolyn Hester?*

Nanci Griffith
1997

photo by
Señor
McGuire

247

Nanci: Exactly! But maybe we can provide the wings through this song, this album.

Joe: *Peter, Paul and Mary certainly took flight with this song in the early sixties.*

Nanci: I remember that Peter, Paul and Mary had the hit with "If I Had a Hammer" in the early sixties because the Weavers had long since been black-listed during the McCarthy era.

Joe: *On the subject of blacklisting, do you see the irony in the fact that Elvis Presley, for example, is celebrated as a rebel, partly because he was censored from the waist down on* The Ed Sullivan Show *in the 1950s, whereas Pete Seeger was totally banned from the same show because of his left-wing politics and songs?*

Nanci: Maybe not then, but now I certainly do see the irony in all this. Pete and many others were told that anything they had to sing, speak, or say on any matter was not permissible on the American airwaves. The Everlys' "Wake Up Little Susie" was banned in New England, as was Buddy Holly and the Crickets' "Midnight Shift" and "Peggy Sue." Little Richard was also banned.

It was so bad that a TV program in the sixties called *Hootenanny* had many people on its blacklist, including Pete Seeger, the Weavers, and Phil Ochs. Carolyn Hester knows much more about this than I do. She refused to cooperate with the system. *Hootenanny* was supposed to be championing folk music, but that list of artists who were blacklisted was so extensive that children were denied, for example, the original version of "If I Had a Hammer" by its author, Pete Seeger, for ten years. Likewise the whole of America. But then, that McCarthy scourge was a disgrace, a real violation of human rights in America. Anyone who was suspected of having left-wing leanings was hounded, or named by cowards like John Wayne, who didn't wait to be called by the House Un-American Activities Committee, he just volunteered information.

Joe: *Why does that make John Wayne a coward?*

Nanci: Because he testified against fellow actors, producers, writers, and in that sense, he turned in other people, though no one ever says that about the Duke. But he was a coward in that respect. He went gung ho for naming names. That's why people who took a stand against that committee, like Humphrey Bogart and Lauren Bacall, weren't ever again friends with the Duke. He was a hypocrite, too, appearing in all those war movies, when he never even fought in the war. And he made all those anti-Commie movies in the 1950s. That's how he felt, and he did what he thought was right, but sadly, more often than not it's still that aspect of America that is celebrated, and anyone opposed to that is frowned upon, as Pete Seeger was. I'm pretty sure some people in positions of power still see Pete Seeger as a "Commie" and would blacklist him if they could. But, to me, Pete Seeger is far more of a true American hero than John Wayne.

Joe: *Were your mother and father considered subversive in the 1950s?*

Nanci: McCarthyism touched Washington, New York, and Los Angeles, where it was assumed the power was. I don't think the committee was after people in Texas.

Joe: *So the Hollywood Ten could have gone to Texas and made all the movies they wanted?*

Nanci: They still could!

Joe: *On the level of its lyrics, what, exactly, does "If I Had a Hammer" mean to you, particularly as we move into a new millennium?*

Nanci: It's about declaring your love for humankind. It's all about humanity, saving precious values, passing them on—which is what this record is all about! Those lessons surely are the best we can bring into a new century. That's why I see "If I Had a Hammer" as an anthem, one of the greatest songs ever written. In those days before political correctness, Pete Seeger and Lee Hays wrote, "I'd hammer out the love between my brothers all over this land." They didn't say "sisters," though they meant everyone. But Pete always says "brothers and sisters" now.

It's so lovely to close the album with it, have all of us in that first verse.

Pete Seeger at home
1958

photo by
David Gahr

Rosalie Sorrels
NEW YORK, 1996

photo by Alan Messer

Eric Weissberg, Nanci
Griffith in background
NEW YORK, 1996

"If I Had a Hammer"
photo by Alan Messer

Lee Hays
NEW YORK, 1958

photo by David Gahr

251

Nanci Griffith and Jay Joyce
Nashville vocal session for
"If I Had a Hammer"
NOVEMBER 1996

photo by
Alan Messer

Gillian Welch
Overdub session for
"If I Had a Hammer"
NASHVILLE, 1996

photo by Alan Messer

And then to have Rosalie Sorrels and Gillian Welch and Odetta, three generations of women, singing, "If I had a bell, if I had a song." And to have all those punk boys there, like Richard Thompson. And when that verse comes in with those boys, they are absolutely stunning.

Joe: *Men, Nanci.*

Nanci: Right! They are men but you can't help but call them the punk boys: Matthew Ryan, Jay Joyce, Richard Thompson, Glen Phillips—all of those guys are punk boys to their souls. And it's amazing how Richard Thompson comes in there and gives them dignity because you can then understand the lyric! Without his voice I don't think you would have been able to understand it! Those boys were way out where the buses don't run! He came in and gathered the troops. But then he is the king of those punk boys!

Then we come back with everybody at the end, which is exactly how it should be. We wanted Pete Seeger to be there, but he was involved in a children's program in New York City and couldn't get away. But to have Eric Weissberg there was so wonderful—the next best thing.

Joe: *"If I had a song" is a pivotal line to start saying good-bye with, isn't it?*

Nanci: Absolutely. That's where the album ends. And that's exactly what both albums of *Other Voices* are all about. It is saying to people, "Here is your song. Sing it out. Pass it on."

---

same song, same voice

A n o t h e r   p e r s p e c t i v e :
Nanci listening to playback

[*Responding to chorus, first time*] This has to be the closure! Come on out, boys! As I said, punk voices pulled back from the brink by the dignity of Richard Thompson! There really is no other way this album could end. I love "If I Had a Hammer," and I love it when Gillian's voice comes in. In fact, the communal spirit of this song is precisely what this and the first *Other Voices* album really, really are both all about.

When those boys come in, it's like "Oh, look who you've woken up!" as if they've been asleep throughout the whole record! Hopefully, that's a metaphor for all the people we will wake up to the fact of how great folk music is, after they hear *Other Voices, Too: The Trip Back to Bountiful.* I really hope that is what happens in the immediate future and long after I have handed over this hammer for the last time.

‖∶   s a m e   s o n g ,   a n o t h e r   v o i c e   ∶‖

JIM ROONEY

This, of course, is one of *the* big folk anthems. We all feel that Pete Seeger has contributed enormously to what we do and helped create an environment where this kind of music is possible. He's a remarkable man, and this song has a message. Some people say, "Why not give it a rest?" but that's another characteristic in Nanci that I admire: she will not give this song a rest. She wants to keep after people to focus on what is important here: justice, brotherhood, all these platitudes that people mouth.

The reality of these concepts is very difficult to implement in people's lives, and if you don't pay attention, you wind up with injustice and no

Dublin sessions

1 9 9 7

photo by
Gerry O'Leary

brotherhood and a lot of hate and a lot of fear. And you have to keep fighting for these values. That's why we wanted to close this album with "If I Had a Hammer." A single song can play a part in giving people a sense of awareness along these lines. Single songs certainly have, in my life. I'm not a demonstrative person. I don't like to parade myself, so I have to deal with things in my own life and do work that I hope will lead people to a better way of living. And I like being involved in records and being involved with artists, because I do want to help make people's lives better. That's the best we can do. If we're given an opportunity to reach people, where people are buying a record or a book, we want that to make their lives better, not worse. Trying to be helpful, even along those lines, is what it's all about, to me.

With albums like *Other Voices, Other Rooms* we are trying to help people celebrate their lives through music and get a voice of their own. There is nothing better than having a voice of your own. When you know that you can say what you feel, in your heart and say it with a certain style and conviction, you're doing something really worthwhile. You're *living*. Muddy Waters once told me, "I wanted to be somebody. I wanted to be a known person." All the people we work with on this album are somebody. They have become somebody because they have been open to life and have responded to it in a positive way.

same song, another voice

MATTHEW RYAN

It was such a thrill for me to sing a verse in this, along with people like Richard Thompson and Jay Joyce. I was very naive about who was there, but what struck me was that there were people who were in their fifties and sixties, and I'm twenty-five, one of the youngest people there. So it was such a cross-section of generations there, which is pretty appropriate for this particular song, isn't it? But because I am from a younger generation, what it all did for me was introduce me to folk music at this level.

My grandfather used to sing all these songs that would blow me away, but I never knew where those old folk songs came from. And you don't read about this in rock magazines, right? So to actually meet these artists and realize that they wrote and recorded a lot of those songs that were part of my family background—that was really like culture shock!

It was great. Like being in a dream state, like saying, "When the hell am I going to wake up here?" I mean, I'm just getting comfortable being around Nanci, writing with her, and then suddenly I'm in the company of all these heavyweights! It was surreal! Though it probably blew me away more *after* I did the sessions. For ages afterward I just kept looking back and thinking, "Did I really take part in all that?"

And that song itself is so good. It's timeless. Not just a song of freedom but a song of communality, understanding, beyond the fact that you're Irish, I'm American, whatever. It's about acceptance. And that's why I really can get into the center of that line I sing: "If I had a song, I'd sing it in the morning." And if Nanci says that's where she wants the album to end, at that line, that's really something special to me.

Nanci really has that kind of faith in me, probably more faith than I have in myself. I imagine she sees something in me that I will one day see. That's why to be involved in this project meant the world to me.

Rosalie Sorrels and Matthew Ryan
NEW YORK, 1996

"If I Had a Hammer"
photo by
Alan Messer

coda:
pete seeger

This phone conversation between Joe Jackson and Pete Seeger took place in late February 1998. The eighty-year-old Pete Seeger was not only gracious with his time but also articulate, forceful, focused, and, well, no less than what one would expect from a man many describe as the father of modern folk music and the person Nanci Griffith calls a true American hero. Pete Seeger is also a teacher in the purest possible sense. He lives to impart the knowledge he has amassed.

Pete: Nanci Griffith's a magnificent artist. I was delighted with her version of the "Hammer" song. I haven't heard her version of "Wimoweh" because although it was sent to me I mislaid the tape. Sorry!

Joe: *You are a presence that weaves its way in and out of the book at seminal moments, so I'd like to give readers a musical and political context for your work, if I may, though both aspects, obviously, are interrelated. Nanci and I talk about the fact that Elvis is celebrated as a pop rebel because he was "banned from the waist down" on* The Ed Sullivan Show *in the 1950s, but you were banned from the brain down—totally censored.*

Pete Seeger
CLEAR-
WATER
FESTIVAL,
1982

*photo by
David Gahr*

257

Pete: That is true! I was banned from TV and radio and commercial-type jobs, but I didn't depend on these things. I sang in schools and summer camps and peace demonstrations and union meetings. And whenever I needed money I could sing at a college. They'd sell tickets, and I'd get a thousand dollars. So the whole situation was a joke. When the authorities in television or radio or wherever would criticize me, all they did was give me free publicity. For example, when a concert would not sell out, my manager would say, "Gee, Pete, we should have gotten the John Birch Society to attack you. Then we would have sold all the tickets!"

Joe: *But there is also a serious subtext to all this. You were not allowed to sing, on television, the original versions of songs like "If I Had a Hammer" because they were deemed anti-American or socialist. So much for freedom of expression in the "land of the free."*

Pete: That's right. I didn't get any job on television for seventeen years, from roughly the early 1950s until 1968. And that was because of my left-wing politics, totally.

Joe: *Going straight to the people is a process that somehow seems more pure to you. Didn't you once tell your fans not to buy your records? That is* really *subversive and must have made you the absolute darling of the record industry!*

Pete: [*Laughing*] Yes. I'm sure it did. But the point is that my whole purpose in being a musician is to put songs on people's lips, not in their ears. And while the record can help people learn music, I actually feel happiest when I hear people singing my songs, not listening to them.

Joe: *Nanci says she hooked into folk music not only because her parents were listening to people like you but also because she came of age at a time when guys like Buddy Holly and the Crickets were starting out. Jim Rooney also claims that the work of those early rockabilly and rock and roll stars should now be seen as folk music. Would you go along with that?*

Pete: In a sense, yes, depending on how you want to stretch the term. You can say that rock and roll is the folk music of the second half of the twentieth century. In fact, I had a friend who said that jazz was the folk music of cities like Memphis and New Orleans. Of course the term "folk music" was first used in the nineteenth century by people in Europe, and the word "volk" meant "people" in German. But it was a German who coined the term *Volksmusik,* and he meant the music of the peasants, ancient and anonymous. Whereas music of the cities, played by people in the market-place was pop music, and music in the castle was fine arts music. All around the world you find these three types of music.

But there's one example that can really bring this into focus and is, quite frankly, a better definition of "folk music." The Gamelan orchestras play the fine arts music of Indonesia but they also play pop music, which was a mix-ture of Dutch and Indonesian. And they also had some very ancient folk songs, which mothers had sung to their children for uncounted generations. That, to me, is folk music. All three forms as one: music of the people.

Joe: *So you don't buy into the purist line on folk music?*

Pete: I don't bother with purists in terms of anything! But overall I try to avoid the use of the phrase "folk music." You're going to be using it in this book but if anybody calls me a folksinger, I point out that I'm not a folk-singer.

Joe: *Why?*

Pete: Because I sing pop songs. I sing George Gershwin and Irving Berlin. And I occasionally sing a little Bach or Beethoven. I mix all forms. So what does that make me? A pop singer? A fine arts singer? I'll tell you what: if you must label me, call me a river singer, because I sing up and down the Hudson River!

Joe: *When Nanci talks about why she brought "Wimoweh" back to its original version, she does highlight the tensions between folk and pop in American music. Basically she describes the pop version as a violation of the original song and says that's why she insisted on restoring the song's original meaning.*

Pete: Well, I'm very glad to hear that.

Joe: *Tell me what "Wimoweh" means—originally meant—to you.*

Pete: I would like to point out that it was the hit song in Johannesburg in 1939. In fact, it was so popular that a batch of imitation songs like it were sold in the 1940s. And it was in 1949 that a batch of these songs were sent from Johannesburg to Decca Records, hoping they could sell in this country. Decca took one listen, said, "Nothing commercial here," and they were going to throw them out.

But a friend of mine, folklorist Alan Lomax, was working at Decca, and he said, "I thought you might like to listen to these." And I was fascinated and found one song that had only one word in it—"Wimoweh"—and I thought, "Shucks, I can learn this!" I didn't realize there was an extra phrase I should have learned. It was in Zulu. It says, "*You* are a lion"—as in, *the people* are a lion. The spirit of Shaka is in the people, but the lion is sleeping.

Joe: *That is the political and spiritual context Nanci gives to the song.*

Pete: Good. Good. Incidentally, following the success of "Wimoweh," by the Weavers, I met the head of the African company that had originally published the song. He came to New York again, to see if he could drum up some business. I said, "Do the Africans ever try and put political words in their songs?" He said, "They *try* it all the time, but we weed it out." Well, he obviously missed this one!

Joe: *As a person who has remained politically active throughout your lifetime, from what is largely perceived as a left-wing perspective, would you have any problem with the fact that artists such as Nanci Griffith focus more on personal concerns, though, obviously in her case, not exclusively?*

Pete: No. This is normal. It's been done throughout history. People feel like writing poetry or songs when they go through a crisis. That's the bottom line, whether that is a war or, say, a strike, which, in a sense, is a local war. But people also feel compelled to write when they fall in love or when somebody you love dies. Or when you travel to a new place, like when the Americans went from the East to the West and we had all sorts of songs written about covered wagons—some sad, because people were leaving home and thinking, "Remember the Red River Valley."

Likewise, nowadays, in this modern world everybody is facing crises in their own lives. Nothing is definite anymore. The old church things don't seem to make as much sense as they once did. But people are not quite sure what new idea is right for them.

Uncertainty dominates the times we live in. People change their minds. But then, I've changed my mind a whole lot of times. Back in the 1930s I went along with friends who said, "Surely the Soviet Union is going to show the world the right way to live." Of course, by the 1950s it became apparent that there were too many mistakes being made, too many crimes perpetrated in the name of socialism.

Then in the 1960s I changed my mind again because I disagreed with those who said change would come about if we all just focused on youth, on the young population at the time. There were too many people like me, who were not exactly young, who were never going to go along with that. So this, to me, was one of the great failings of the sixties generation. They were too self-centered, too youth-oriented. I never wanted my audience to be exclusive in any way. I love my audience to be two or three or more generations out there. To have grandparents, parents, kids. But I really do believe that's where the sixties failed, and let's face it, groups like the Beatles were part of that.

Joe: *As was Dylan, obviously, whether you see the sixties, politically, as a success or a failure. He certainly alienated many people at that legendary Newport Folk Festival. Jim Rooney talks about when Dylan went electric and, it's said, folk-rock was born. Jim suggests you were opposed to what Dylan was doing because you thought he was playing too loud. Is that true?*

Pete: It's true that I've never played very loud music. I like steel drums! That's about the only type of music I can play loud! But I prefer acoustic instruments. On the other hand, we had lots of electric instruments at Newport.

Joe: *The Paul Butterfield Blues Band who played just before Dylan!*

Pete: Exactly. And Howlin' Wolf and Muddy Waters. But I made a big mistake that night. I was the emcee, and I could easily have gotten onstage and said, "Hey, if you booed Bob, why didn't you boo Howlin' Wolf yesterday? Why didn't you boo Muddy Waters last year?" I should have said, "Bob's got a right to electrify if he wants to." And actually, when it all happened, he was playing one of his absolutely best songs, "Ain't Gonna Work on Maggie's Farm No More."

Joe: *Which is a song of both personal and political protest.*

Pete: Very much. So it wasn't the song I was complaining about, or the electrification. I was complaining about the fact that you could not hear the words. The distortion was such that you could not understand a single word he was saying. I ran over to the guys in charge of the sound, and I said, "Fix up the sound so the audience can understand the words," and they hollered back, "This is the way they want it." And I said, "God damn it, if I had an ax I'd cut the cable right now!"

Joe: *That's one hell of a mystery in pop culture solved right there! So it wasn't the fact that Dylan went electric in Newport that upset you. It was the fact that the electrical distortion drowned out the words?*

Pete: Absolutely. But people really have misunderstood that over the years since then. I was upset simply because I felt that the audience couldn't hear those great lyrics Bob was singing in "Maggie's Farm." That's all.

Joe: *Nanci said she's doing these albums partly because one of her earliest memories is waking up as a child and hearing her father playing records by the Weavers on his hi-fi. That's a pretty symbolic wake-up call, don't you think?*

Pete: I guess it is!

Joe: *She says she's recording these albums to bring things full circle. That's also why she ends the new album with "If I Had a Hammer," though of course she's also saying, "Take this hammer and pass it on."*
In that sense isn't Nanci being true to your core belief: "Take this song, put it on the lips of people, maybe even on the lips of a new generation"?

Pete: Absolutely. As in "Pass it on." The human race has been doing it for hundreds of thousands of years. And if we do our job right, the songs will still be here a thousand years from now.

But I'm not really such an optimist. When people ask me, "Do you really think you can clean up the Hudson?" I say, "In a hundred, two hundred years, this river is going to be so clean you can drink out of it."

I'll tell you how I'm so certain we'll clean up the Hudson and get rid of militarism, racism, sexism, poverty amid plenty, and a whole lot of other stupid things. Because if we don't, there will be no human race here, and that river will be clean as a whistle.

Joe: *That seems to sum up the ambivalence that some say sits at the soul of Pete Seeger. Is it true that there has always been this tension in your life between the better world you sing about and the frustration you feel, deep down, because you know that, really, songs, on their own, don't change anything?*

Pete: Well, I have to face up to the fact that, at times, being optimistic means that you are just another Pollyanna. As in thinking "Everything's going to be all right" or "God is on our side."

Joe: *Isn't that exactly what Lillian Hellman said to you at one point back in the sixties, when she was mocking your faith in the song "We Shall Overcome," telling you this idea of "Someday it will all happen" was, politically, just infantile "namby-pamby" stuff, unreal to a ridiculous degree?*

Pete: Yeah. She said, "What kind of a revolutionary song is that?" As in "someday, someday, someday." And, in ways, I now see that she was right.

Joe: *But didn't you yourself once write a deeply personal song in which you addressed this very tension between utopian ideals and the reality of what actually can be, or has been, achieved? As in the song "False from True," where you say, "When my song turns to ashes on my tongue and I look in the mirror and see I'm no longer young, then I got to start the job of separating false from true." With all due respect, you now are no longer young, so is this whole question now central to your life, as you look back?*

Pete: And look forward. Of course it is. But not just now. It has been for years, even since before I wrote that song. But it's really ironic that you would quote "False from True," because it has only recently been recorded by a great blues singer called Guy Davis, on Appleseed Records, a small label that has released this album of people singing my songs, called *Where Have All the Flowers Gone?*

Up till now nobody but me had ever sung "False from True." I wrote it in 1968, after Martin Luther King Jr. and Robert Kennedy were assassinated and the Soviet tanks rolled into Prague. And, yes, definitely, "False from True" is central to a key question I've had to confront for much of my life.

Joe: *As in forever reaching for an ideal while trying to live with the pain of knowing that this ideal will probably never be realized?*

Pete: Absolutely. That about says it all.

Joe: *But you still sing and perform?*

Pete: I don't sing much. I haven't much of a voice left. But I'm a song leader. Do you understand that term?

Joe: *I do. Like someone who leads the hymns in church?*

Pete: Right. So I'll say, for example, "Somewhere over the Rainbow," and the whole crowd will sing that line. Then I say "way up high," and they follow me on that. Then they follow me on "there's a land that I heard of once in a lullaby." I just shout out the words, and the crowd sings them.

Joe: *So you're still putting songs on the lips of people who need to sing.*

Pete: I would hope so. But to tell you the truth, I change two words near the end of "Somewhere over the Rainbow." I tell the audience, "There's two more lines to this song, but I had to change the words." And somewhere up there I hear Yip [E. Y. Harburg, the song's composer] saying, "Pete, you can mess around with your old folk songs, but don't start messing with 'Somewhere over the Rainbow,' please!" But I look up to heaven and say, "Yip, wherever you are, I've got to change two words because if I was there when thirteen-year-old Dorothy was saying, "Bluebirds fly over the rainbow, why, oh, why can't I?" I'd say, "I'll tell you why you can't: because you're only thinking of yourself. You've got to ask for this dream to come true for everybody. You've got to believe that we're all going to make it over that rainbow or nobody's going to make it."

So I get these people to sing, "If happy little bluebirds fly above the rainbow, why can't you and I?" And the whole crowd sings it with these words!

Joe: *I'd like to bring us back to the closing track on Nanci's album, "If I Had a Hammer," which she describes as a song about declaring your love for humankind. Jim Rooney describes it as one of the great anthems of our time. Do you see it as such?*

Pete: It sure has proved itself to be that, so far, though I don't know if it will last another century. After all, carpenters don't use hammers anymore! They use pneumatic drills!

Joe: *Which is hardly an easy phrase to rhyme! Somehow "If I Had a Pneumatic Drill" doesn't seem quite the same, does it?*

Pete: Not at all. And it'd be far more difficult to sing!

Joe: *Jim Rooney also cites your belief that good music can only do good, whether it rhymes or not. Is that still your belief?*

Pete: Yes. And I hope it is still true—though, as I say, you can't prove a goddamn thing is this world!

Joe: *But you can hope?*

Pete: Definitely. That is what it's all about.

Joe: *So as someone who believes that change begins at a micro rather than a macro level, with individuals and small groups rather than with larger organizations such as political parties, which you've said are too often interested only in power, do you believe that passing on these songs, as Nanci is doing, will work at this fundamental level? Will it initiate change and fire hope?*

Pete: Yeah. I absolutely do. That's why I like this version of "If I Had a Hammer" so much, because I believe that at least some of Nanci's listeners will say, "Oh, boy, this old song has come to life again."

Joe: *Does that mean you believe that the pop versions killed the song?*

Pete: Well, there always is that tendency in pop music to do what you are paid to do without questioning it. But Nanci does bring the song back to its roots, and I would hope that when people hear her version, they really will get what the song is all about. In the end, it is about passing songs on to a new generation, passing on the dreams of those who do believe that humankind can, finally, be united.

Joe: *That leads to one last question. You did say earlier that the tone of the times we live in is one of uncertainty and that this condition is rooted partly in the fact that our faith in God has been fragmented. So when you lead those people through "Somewhere over the Rainbow," where, exactly, are you hoping to take them? Where, in heaven or on this earth, does Pete Seeger most often encounter God? After all, from the beginning of time, whether it was folk, pop, or fine arts–based, music has been seen, ultimately, as a means by which man can reach God, either "out there" or within oneself.*

Pete: It is. But the best definition of God I have comes from A. N. Whitehead, who was a friend of Bertrand Russell's. He wrote a great essay called "The Aims of Education," and I've memorized a few paragraphs of it:

> *When one considers, in its length and in its breadth, the importance of this question of the education of a nation's young, the broken lives, the defeated hopes, the national failures which result from the frivolous inertia, with which it is treated, it is difficult to stifle within one's self a savage rage.*
>
> *In the condition of modern life, the rule is absolute. The nation that does not value trained intelligence is doomed. Not all your heroism, not all your social charm, not all your wit, not all your victories on land and sea can turn back the finger of fate. Today we maintain ourselves, tomorrow science has moved forward another step and there will be no*

appeal from the judgment of history upon the uneducated. Of course education should be religious. This is the aim of education throughout the ages because education should inculcate both duty and reverence.

Duty arises from our potential control over the course of events and where available information could have changed the issue. Ignorance has the guilt of vice. The source of reverence lies in this perception: that the rest holds within itself the complete sum of existence, that great amplitude of time, forward and back, which is eternity.

And I say, if *that* can't make you reverent what the hell would?

Joe: *In other words, in his own sweet and simple way, A. N. Whitehead was saying he believes in God? And that he believes God can be reached through ridding the world of ignorance—that education is, by its very nature, religious?*

Pete: Yes, that about sums it up and says what I feel in relation to God and music and education.

Joe: *It's not the snappiest definition of God I've ever heard, but I hope it will apply, to whatever degree, to Nanci's interpretation of "If I Had a Hammer," the album* Other Voices, Too, *and maybe even this book.*

Pete: I hope so. Because that, to me, is what music and life is all about.

Joe: *Okay, I will pass that on.*

Pete: It is worth passing, don't you think?

Joe: *Absolutely. Thank you. For everything.*

index